A POSITIVE THINKING, MINDFULNESS AND WELLBEING JOURNAL FOR KIDS AND TEENAGERS

Copyright © 2019 Steve Turner (alias Squidoodle).
The rights of Steve Turner (Squidoodle) to be identified as the illustrator of this work has been asserted by him in accordance with the Copyright, Designs and Patents Act 1988.
All rights reserved, including the right of reproduction in whole or in any part in any form.

There's no RIGHT way and no WRONG way to work in this journal. Fill it in daily, fill it in weekly or fill it in whenever you feel like it.

But don't let it stress you - no-one is making you do it everyday.

The idea is to **find something positive** and record it... that way you can think about it while you write it and remember it when you need to... **and maybe that will help.**

put the date here

everyone loves a good quote right?

this bit is obvious :)

CIRCLE THE EMOJI THAT BEST DESCRIBES HOW YOU FELT TODAY

tick where you are on the kindness tracker - no matter how small the act of kindness :)

you know when you can't stop thinking about something? write it here....

this bit is obvious as well ... and it doesn't have to be something big and important

use this dot grid to make lists, draw scrolls, boxes and more. Then you can add lists and things to remember.

Tick a box on the good things checklist!

TIME TO GET CREATIVE IN THIS BOX – DOODLE A THING OR A PATTERN!

if something is worrying you, write it in the worry monster's mouth!

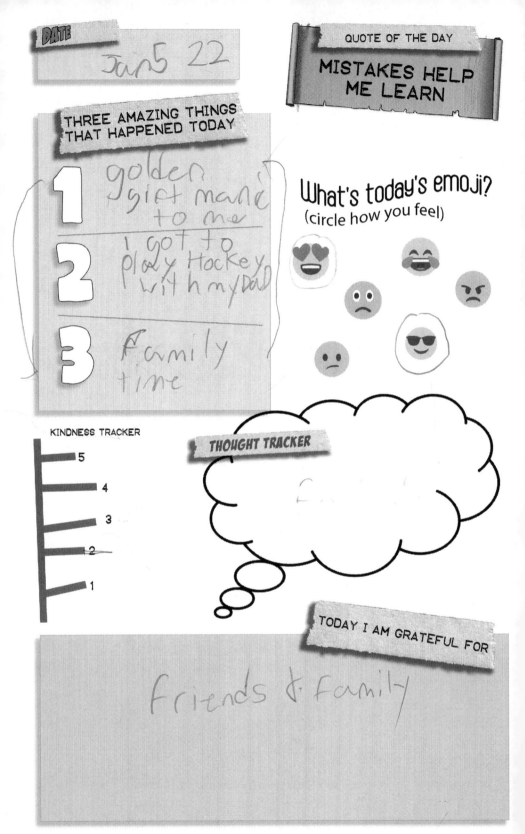

DATE Jan5 22

QUOTE OF THE DAY
MISTAKES HELP ME LEARN

THREE AMAZING THINGS THAT HAPPENED TODAY

1 golden gift made to me

2 i got to play Hockey with my Dad

3 Family time

What's today's emoji?
(circle how you feel)

KINDNESS TRACKER

5
4
3
2
1

THOUGHT TRACKER

TODAY I AM GRATEFUL FOR

Friends & Family

Fnc5

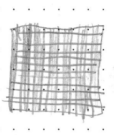

THE GOOD THINGS CHECKLIST

- [ ] I TIDIED SOMETHING
- [x] I WAS A GOOD FRIEND
- [x] I SMILED ABOUT SOMETHING
- [ ] I HELPED SOMEONE
- [ ] I HELPED MYSELF
- [x] I TRIED MY HARDEST

FEED THE WORRY MONSTER

Daily Doodle OR pattern

Jan 6 2022

THREE AMAZING THINGS THAT HAPPENED TODAY

1 Watching Kim's convience

2 getting a dub

3 shoveling

What's today's emoji?
(circle how you feel)

KINDNESS TRACKER

5
4
3
2
1

THOUGHT TRACKER

Hockey

TODAY I AM GRATEFUL FOR

Family

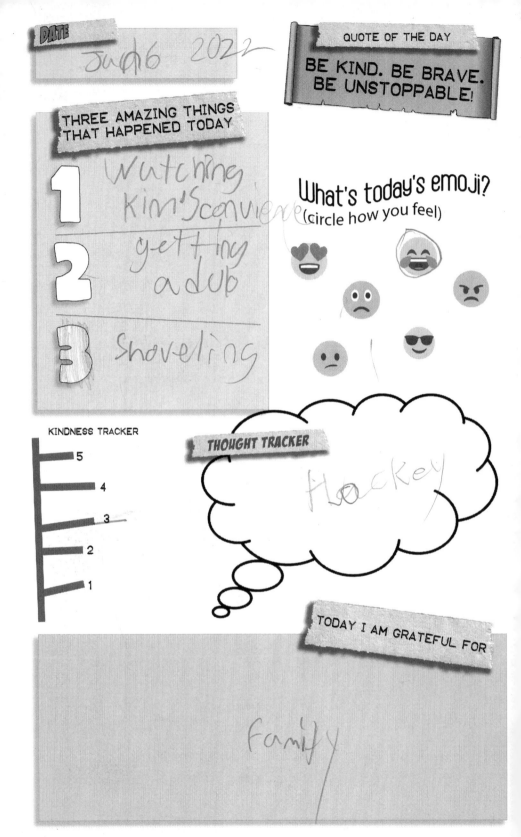

THE GOOD THINGS CHECKLIST

- ☑ I TIDIED SOMETHING
- ☐ I WAS A GOOD FRIEND
- ☑ I SMILED ABOUT SOMETHING
- ☑ I HELPED SOMEONE
- ☑ I HELPED MYSELF
- ☑ I TRIED MY HARDEST

FEED THE WORRY MONSTER

Daily Doodle or Pattern

Jan 7 2022

THREE AMAZING THINGS THAT HAPPENED TODAY

1 Kim's with fam

2 building Lego

3 Play Xbox

What's today's emoji?
(circle how you feel)

KINDNESS TRACKER

5
4
3
2
1

THOUGHT TRACKER

tiktok

TODAY I AM GRATEFUL FOR

Friends

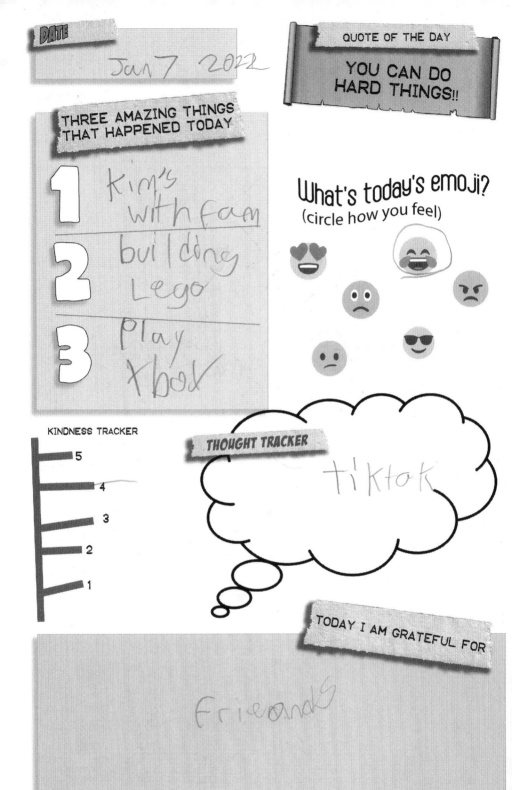

LISTS AND BULLET JOURNAL DESIGNS

THE GOOD THINGS CHECKLIST

- [ ] I TIDIED SOMETHING
- [ ] I WAS A GOOD FRIEND
- [x] I SMILED ABOUT SOMETHING
- [ ] I HELPED SOMEONE
- [x] I HELPED MYSELF
- [x] I TRIED MY HARDEST

FEED THE WORRY MONSTER

Daily Doodle OR pattern

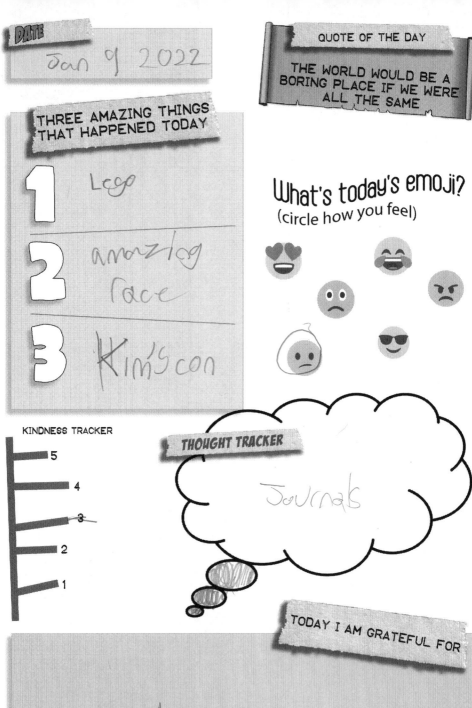

DATE

Jan 9 2022

QUOTE OF THE DAY

THE WORLD WOULD BE A BORING PLACE IF WE WERE ALL THE SAME

THREE AMAZING THINGS THAT HAPPENED TODAY

1 Lego

2 amazing race

3 Kim's con

What's today's emoji?
(circle how you feel)

KINDNESS TRACKER

5
4
3
2
1

THOUGHT TRACKER

Journals

TODAY I AM GRATEFUL FOR

my dog

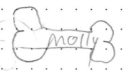

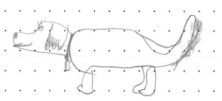

THE GOOD THINGS CHECKLIST

- ☐ I TIDIED SOMETHING
- ☑ I WAS A GOOD FRIEND
- ☑ I SMILED ABOUT SOMETHING
- ☑ I HELPED SOMEONE
- ☑ I HELPED MYSELF
- ☑ I TRIED MY HARDEST

FEED THE WORRY MONSTER

Daily Doodle OR Pattern

DATE
Jan 10 22

QUOTE OF THE DAY
DON'T LET ANYONE DULL YOUR SPARKLE

THREE AMAZING THINGS THAT HAPPENED TODAY

1 seeing my friends

2 getting my book

3 TV time

What's today's emoji?
(circle how you feel)

KINDNESS TRACKER
5
4
3
2
1

THOUGHT TRACKER
books

TODAY I AM GRATEFUL FOR
Scotty

THE GOOD THINGS CHECKLIST

- [ ] I TIDIED SOMETHING
- [x] I WAS A GOOD FRIEND
- [ ] I SMILED ABOUT SOMETHING
- [ ] I HELPED SOMEONE
- [x] I HELPED MYSELF
- [x] I TRIED MY HARDEST

Daily Doodle or Pattern

FEED THE WORRY MONSTER

Jan 11 2024

BE PROUD OF HOW HARD YOU ARE TRYING

THREE AMAZING THINGS THAT HAPPENED TODAY

1 GYM

2 Lego

3 reading

What's today's emoji?
(circle how you feel)

KINDNESS TRACKER

5
4
3
2
1

THOUGHT TRACKER

Lego

TODAY I AM GRATEFUL FOR

Legos

THE GOOD THINGS CHECKLIST

FEED THE WORRY MONSTER

- ☑ I TIDIED SOMETHING
- ☑ I WAS A GOOD FRIEND
- ☑ I SMILED ABOUT SOMETHING
- ☑ I HELPED SOMEONE
- ☐ I HELPED MYSELF
- ☐ I TRIED MY HARDEST

Daily Doodle or pattern

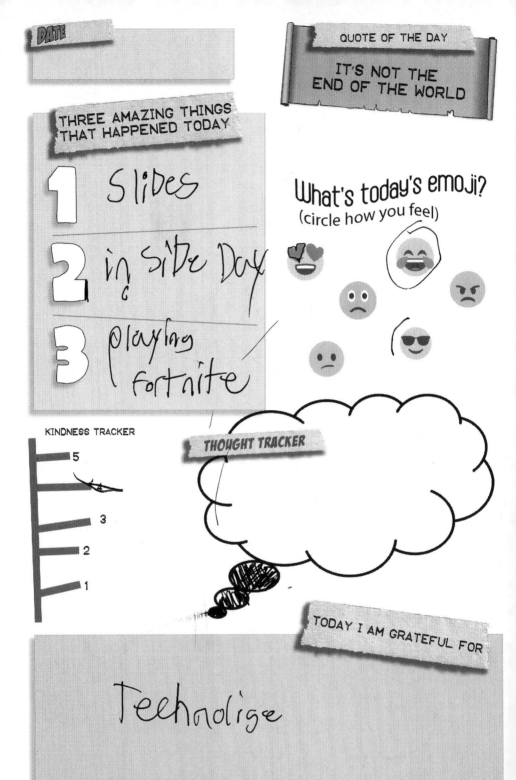

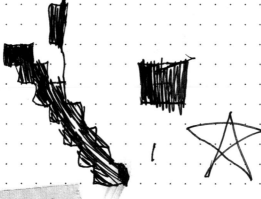

THE GOOD THINGS CHECKLIST

FEED THE WORRY MONSTER

☑ I TIDIED SOMETHING

☑ I WAS A GOOD FRIEND

☑ I SMILED ABOUT SOMETHING

☑ I HELPED SOMEONE

☑ I HELPED MYSELF

☑ I TRIED MY HARDEST

Daily Doodle OR Pattern

THREE AMAZING THINGS
THAT HAPPENED TODAY

1 Lego

2 sportchek

3 games

What's today's emoji?
(circle how you feel)

KINDNESS TRACKER

5
4
3
2
1

THOUGHT TRACKER

Leyo

TODAY I AM GRATEFUL FOR

Agent 13

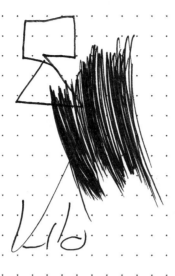

THE GOOD THINGS CHECKLIST

- ☑ I TIDIED SOMETHING
- ☑ I WAS A GOOD FRIEND
- ☑ I SMILED ABOUT SOMETHING
- ☑ I HELPED SOMEONE
- ☐ I HELPED MYSELF
- ☑ I TRIED MY HARDEST

Daily Doodle OR Pattern

FEED THE WORRY MONSTER

Jan 14 2022

QUOTE OF THE DAY

DO WHAT YOU LOVE,
LOVE WHAT YOU DO

THREE AMAZING THINGS THAT HAPPENED TODAY

1 Last Day

2 Friday

3 diner

What's today's emoji?
(circle how you feel)

KINDNESS TRACKER

5
4
3
2
1

THOUGHT TRACKER

novie

TODAY I AM GRATEFUL FOR

Lego

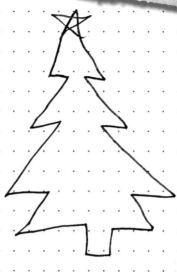

THE GOOD THINGS CHECKLIST

- ☑ I TIDIED SOMETHING
- ☑ I WAS A GOOD FRIEND
- ☑ I SMILED ABOUT SOMETHING
- ☑ I HELPED SOMEONE
- ☑ I HELPED MYSELF
- ☑ I TRIED MY HARDEST

FEED THE WORRY MONSTER

Daily Doodle or Pattern

Jan 16 2022

QUOTE OF THE DAY

NO ACT OF KINDNESS,
NO MATTER HOW SMALL,
IS EVER WASTED.

THREE AMAZING THINGS THAT HAPPENED TODAY

1 Lego

2 Hockey

3 Kim's convience

What's today's emoji?
(circle how you feel)

KINDNESS TRACKER

5
4
3
2
1

THOUGHT TRACKER

steelers

TODAY I AM GRATEFUL FOR

Kimmy Shmit

THE GOOD THINGS CHECKLIST

- [ ] I TIDIED SOMETHING
- [x] I WAS A GOOD FRIEND
- [ ] I SMILED ABOUT SOMETHING
- [ ] I HELPED SOMEONE
- [x] I HELPED MYSELF
- [ ] I TRIED MY HARDEST

FEED THE WORRY MONSTER

Daily Doodle OR Pattern

Jan 28 2022

MAKE SURE YOU ARE HAVING FUN.

THREE AMAZING THINGS THAT HAPPENED TODAY

1 4 Square

2 Lego

3 Science

What's today's emoji?
(circle how you feel)

KINDNESS TRACKER

5
4
3
2
1

THOUGHT TRACKER

Baseball

TODAY I AM GRATEFUL FOR

Friends

LISTS AND BULLET JOURNAL DESIGNS

THE GOOD THINGS CHECKLIST

- [x] I TIDIED SOMETHING
- [x] I WAS A GOOD FRIEND
- [x] I SMILED ABOUT SOMETHING
- [x] I HELPED SOMEONE
- [x] I HELPED MYSELF
- [x] I TRIED MY HARDEST

FEED THE WORRY MONSTER

Daily Doodle OR Pattern

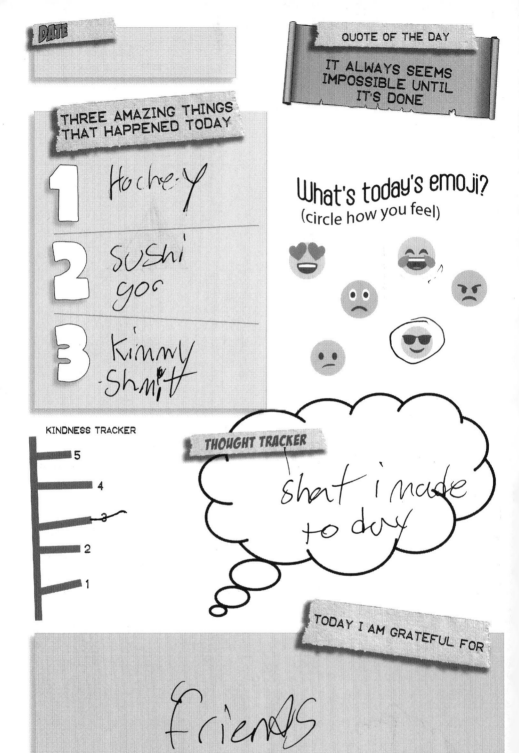

DATE

QUOTE OF THE DAY

IT ALWAYS SEEMS IMPOSSIBLE UNTIL IT'S DONE

THREE AMAZING THINGS THAT HAPPENED TODAY

1 Hockey

2 sushi goo

3 Kimmy Shmit

What's today's emoji?
(circle how you feel)

KINDNESS TRACKER

5
4
3
2
1

THOUGHT TRACKER

shit i made to day

TODAY I AM GRATEFUL FOR

Friends

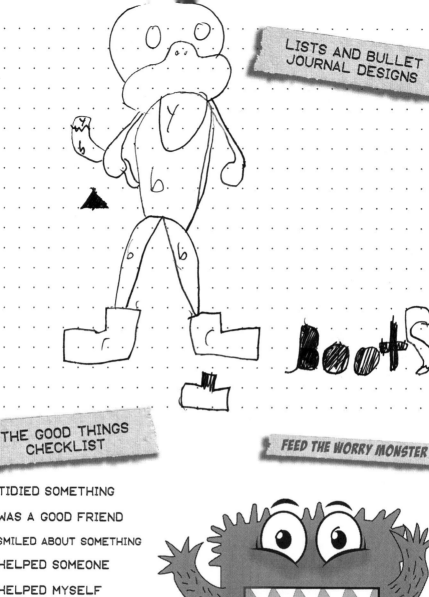

Boots

THE GOOD THINGS CHECKLIST

- 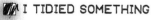 I TIDIED SOMETHING
- I WAS A GOOD FRIEND
- I SMILED ABOUT SOMETHING
- I HELPED SOMEONE
- I HELPED MYSELF
- I TRIED MY HARDEST

FEED THE WORRY MONSTER

Daily Doodle OR pattern

DATE

THREE AMAZING THINGS
THAT HAPPENED TODAY

1

2

3

What's today's emoji?
(circle how you feel)

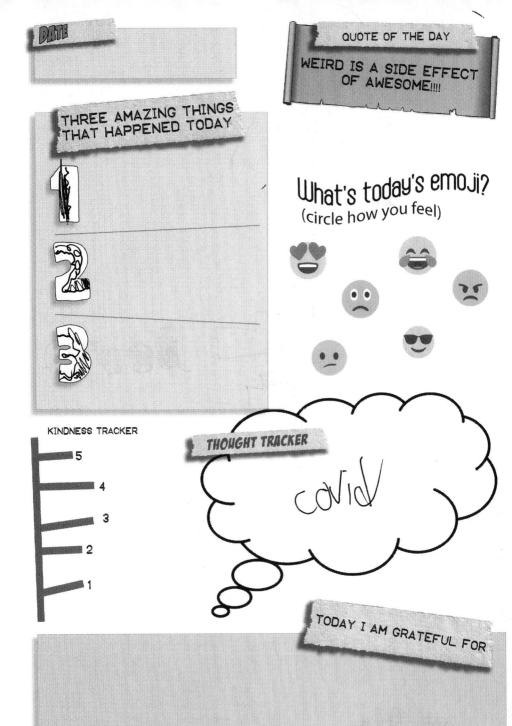

KINDNESS TRACKER

5

4

3

2

1

THOUGHT TRACKER

covid

TODAY I AM GRATEFUL FOR

THE GOOD THINGS CHECKLIST

- [ ] I TIDIED SOMETHING
- [ ] I WAS A GOOD FRIEND
- [ ] I SMILED ABOUT SOMETHING
- [ ] I HELPED SOMEONE
- [ ] I HELPED MYSELF
- [ ] I TRIED MY HARDEST

Daily Doodle OR pattern

FEED THE WORRY MONSTER

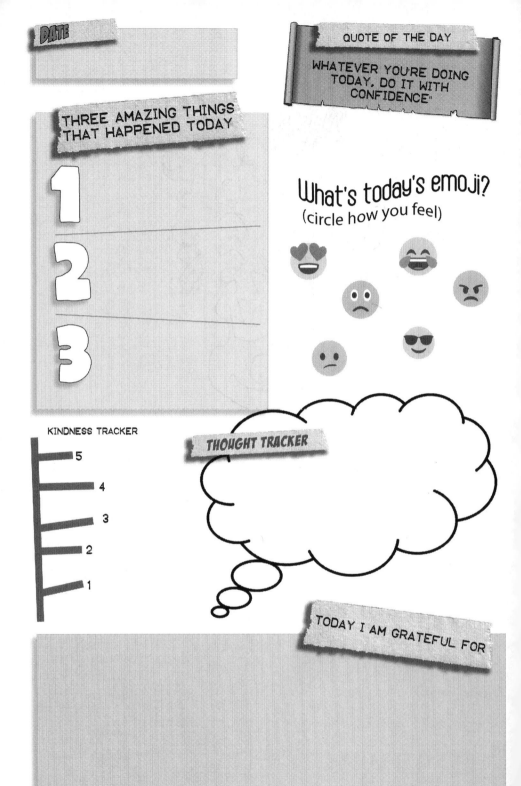

DATE

THREE AMAZING THINGS THAT HAPPENED TODAY

1

2

3

What's today's emoji?
(circle how you feel)

KINDNESS TRACKER

5

4

3

2

1

THOUGHT TRACKER

TODAY I AM GRATEFUL FOR

THE GOOD THINGS CHECKLIST

- ☐ I TIDIED SOMETHING
- ☐ I WAS A GOOD FRIEND
- ☐ I SMILED ABOUT SOMETHING
- ☐ I HELPED SOMEONE
- ☐ I HELPED MYSELF
- ☐ I TRIED MY HARDEST

FEED THE WORRY MONSTER

Daily Doodle OR Pattern

DATE

THREE AMAZING THINGS
THAT HAPPENED TODAY

1 eh BoD

2 Xbox

3 Hardy BOY

What's today's emoji?
(circle how you feel)

KINDNESS TRACKER

5
4
3
2
1

THOUGHT TRACKER

Hockey

TODAY I AM GRATEFUL FOR

Familiy

THE GOOD THINGS CHECKLIST

- ☑ I TIDIED SOMETHING
- ☑ I WAS A GOOD FRIEND
- ☑ I SMILED ABOUT SOMETHING
- ☑ I HELPED SOMEONE
- ☑ I HELPED MYSELF
- ☐ I TRIED MY HARDEST

FEED THE WORRY MONSTER

Daily Doodle OR Pattern

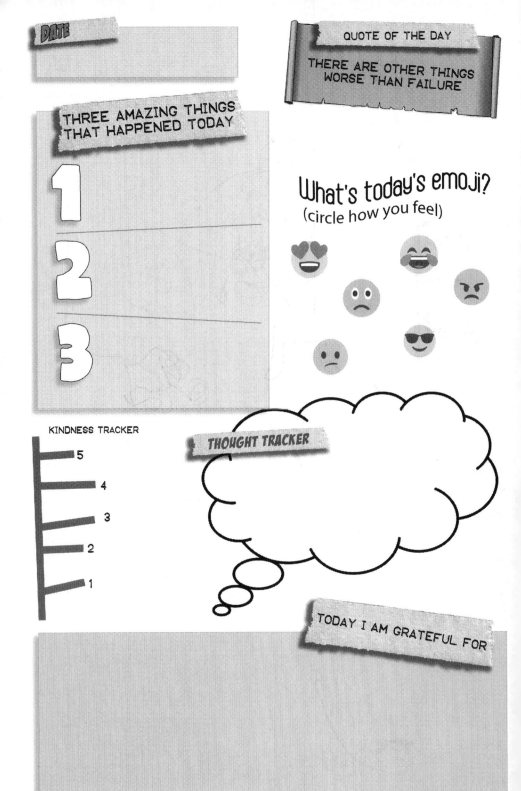

DATE

THREE AMAZING THINGS THAT HAPPENED TODAY

1

2

3

What's today's emoji?
(circle how you feel)

KINDNESS TRACKER

5
4
3
2
1

THOUGHT TRACKER

TODAY I AM GRATEFUL FOR

THE GOOD THINGS CHECKLIST

- [ ] I TIDIED SOMETHING
- [ ] I WAS A GOOD FRIEND
- [ ] I SMILED ABOUT SOMETHING
- [ ] I HELPED SOMEONE
- [ ] I HELPED MYSELF
- [ ] I TRIED MY HARDEST

Daily Doodle OR Pattern

FEED THE WORRY MONSTER

DATE

THREE AMAZING THINGS THAT HAPPENED TODAY

1

2

3

What's today's emoji?
(circle how you feel)

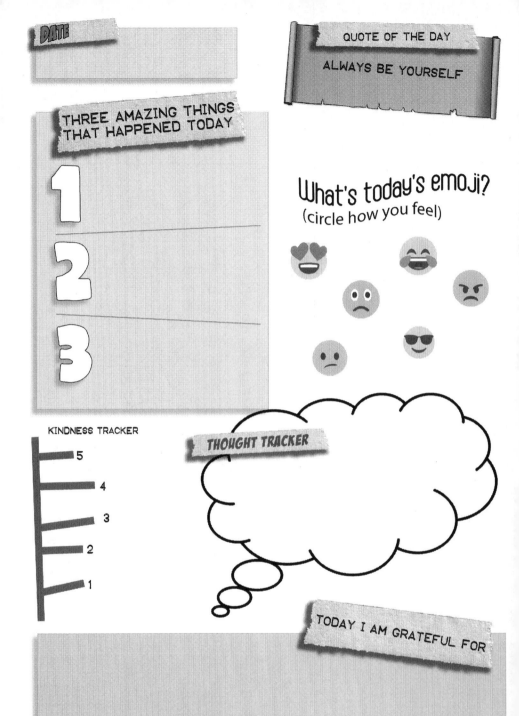

KINDNESS TRACKER

5

4

3

2

1

THOUGHT TRACKER

TODAY I AM GRATEFUL FOR

LISTS AND BULLET JOURNAL DESIGNS

THE GOOD THINGS CHECKLIST

- [ ] I TIDIED SOMETHING
- [ ] I WAS A GOOD FRIEND
- [ ] I SMILED ABOUT SOMETHING
- [ ] I HELPED SOMEONE
- [ ] I HELPED MYSELF
- [ ] I TRIED MY HARDEST

Daily Doodle OR Pattern

FEED THE WORRY MONSTER

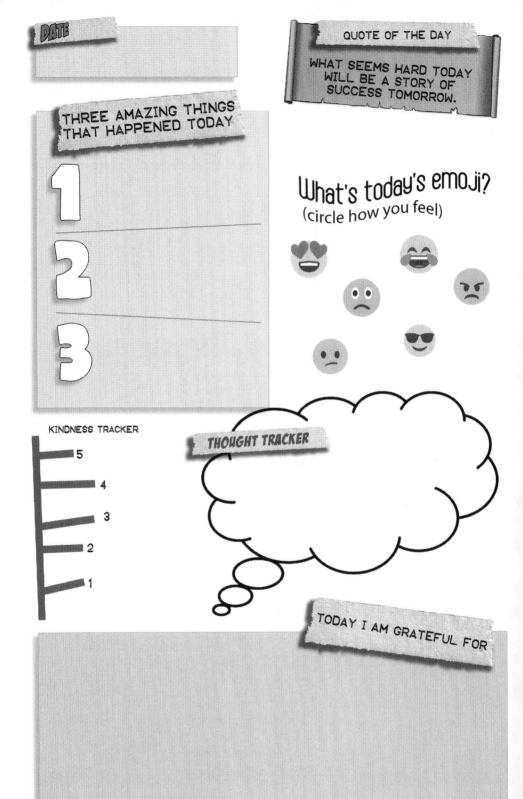

DATE

THREE AMAZING THINGS THAT HAPPENED TODAY

1

2

3

What's today's emoji?
(circle how you feel)

KINDNESS TRACKER

5

4

3

2

1

THOUGHT TRACKER

TODAY I AM GRATEFUL FOR

THE GOOD THINGS
CHECKLIST

FEED THE WORRY MONSTER

- [ ] I TIDIED SOMETHING
- [ ] I WAS A GOOD FRIEND
- [ ] I SMILED ABOUT SOMETHING
- [ ] I HELPED SOMEONE
- [ ] I HELPED MYSELF
- [ ] I TRIED MY HARDEST

Daily Doodle or pattern

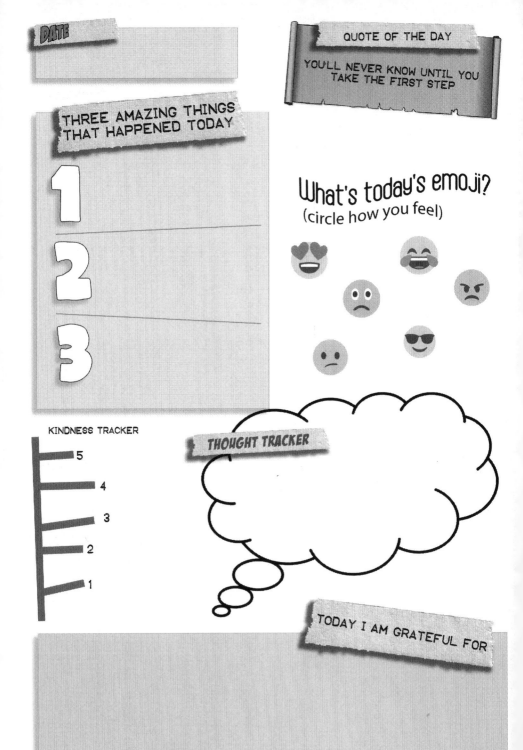

DATE

QUOTE OF THE DAY

YOU'LL NEVER KNOW UNTIL YOU TAKE THE FIRST STEP

THREE AMAZING THINGS THAT HAPPENED TODAY

1

2

3

What's today's emoji?
(circle how you feel)

KINDNESS TRACKER

5

4

3

2

1

THOUGHT TRACKER

TODAY I AM GRATEFUL FOR

THE GOOD THINGS CHECKLIST

FEED THE WORRY MONSTER

- [ ] I TIDIED SOMETHING
- [ ] I WAS A GOOD FRIEND
- [ ] I SMILED ABOUT SOMETHING
- [ ] I HELPED SOMEONE
- [ ] I HELPED MYSELF
- [ ] I TRIED MY HARDEST

Daily Doodle or Pattern

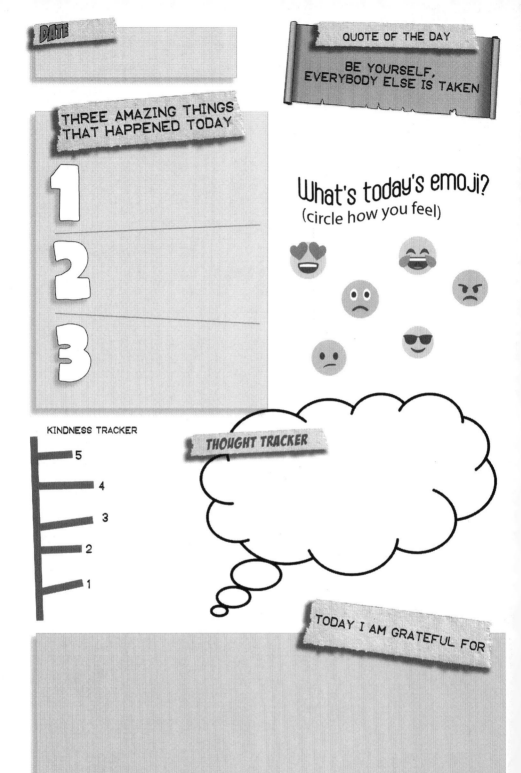

DATE

QUOTE OF THE DAY

BE YOURSELF,
EVERYBODY ELSE IS TAKEN

THREE AMAZING THINGS
THAT HAPPENED TODAY

1

2

3

What's today's emoji?
(circle how you feel)

KINDNESS TRACKER

5

4

3

2

1

THOUGHT TRACKER

TODAY I AM GRATEFUL FOR

THE GOOD THINGS CHECKLIST

- ☐ I TIDIED SOMETHING
- ☐ I WAS A GOOD FRIEND
- ☐ I SMILED ABOUT SOMETHING
- ☐ I HELPED SOMEONE
- ☐ I HELPED MYSELF
- ☐ I TRIED MY HARDEST

Daily Doodle or pattern

FEED THE WORRY MONSTER

CREATE YOUR OWN SUNSHINE

THREE AMAZING THINGS THAT HAPPENED TODAY

1

2

3

What's today's emoji?
(circle how you feel)

KINDNESS TRACKER

5

4

3

2

1

THOUGHT TRACKER

TODAY I AM GRATEFUL FOR

THE GOOD THINGS CHECKLIST

- ☐ I TIDIED SOMETHING
- ☐ I WAS A GOOD FRIEND
- ☐ I SMILED ABOUT SOMETHING
- ☐ I HELPED SOMEONE
- ☐ I HELPED MYSELF
- ☐ I TRIED MY HARDEST

FEED THE WORRY MONSTER

Daily Doodle OR pattern

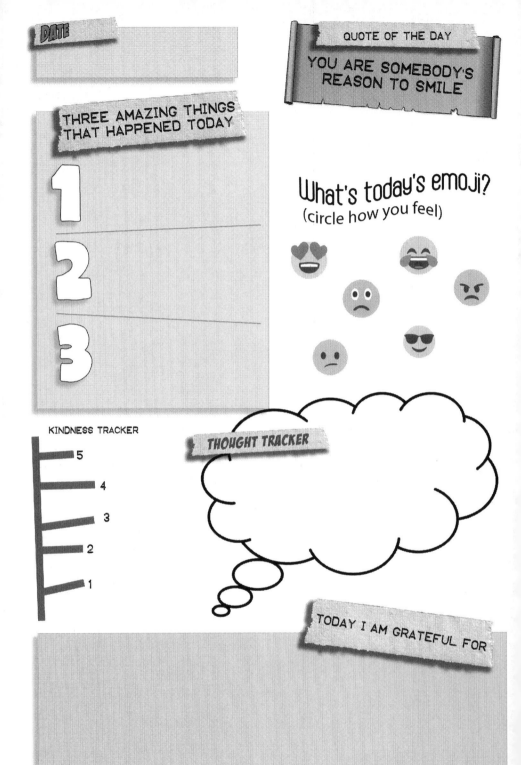

DATE

QUOTE OF THE DAY
YOU ARE SOMEBODY'S REASON TO SMILE

THREE AMAZING THINGS THAT HAPPENED TODAY

1
2
3

What's today's emoji?
(circle how you feel)

KINDNESS TRACKER
5
4
3
2
1

THOUGHT TRACKER

TODAY I AM GRATEFUL FOR

THE GOOD THINGS CHECKLIST

- [ ] I TIDIED SOMETHING
- [ ] I WAS A GOOD FRIEND
- [ ] I SMILED ABOUT SOMETHING
- [ ] I HELPED SOMEONE
- [ ] I HELPED MYSELF
- [ ] I TRIED MY HARDEST

FEED THE WORRY MONSTER

Daily Doodle OR pattern

DATE

A LITTLE PROGRESS
EACH DAY ADDS UP
TO BIG RESULTS

THREE AMAZING THINGS
THAT HAPPENED TODAY

1

2

3

What's today's emoji?
(circle how you feel)

KINDNESS TRACKER

5

4

3

2

1

THOUGHT TRACKER

TODAY I AM GRATEFUL FOR

THE GOOD THINGS CHECKLIST

- [ ] I TIDIED SOMETHING
- [ ] I WAS A GOOD FRIEND
- [ ] I SMILED ABOUT SOMETHING
- [ ] I HELPED SOMEONE
- [ ] I HELPED MYSELF
- [ ] I TRIED MY HARDEST

Daily Doodle OR Pattern

FEED THE WORRY MONSTER

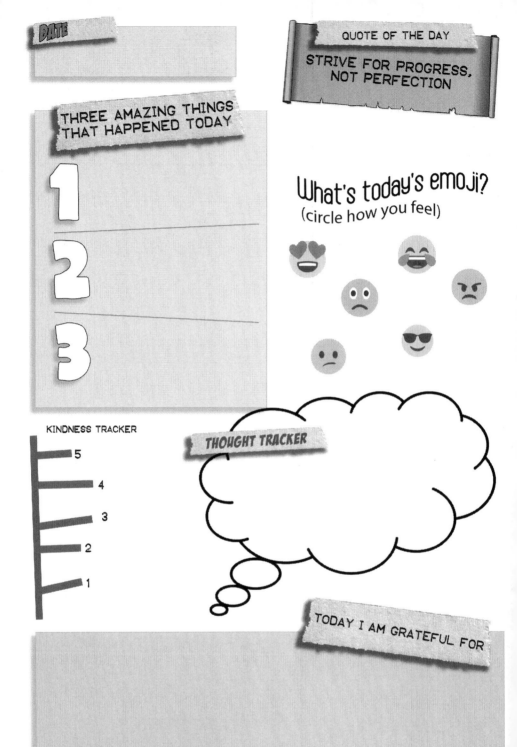

THE GOOD THINGS CHECKLIST

☐ I TIDIED SOMETHING

☐ I WAS A GOOD FRIEND

☐ I SMILED ABOUT SOMETHING

☐ I HELPED SOMEONE

☐ I HELPED MYSELF

☐ I TRIED MY HARDEST

Daily Doodle or Pattern

FEED THE WORRY MONSTER

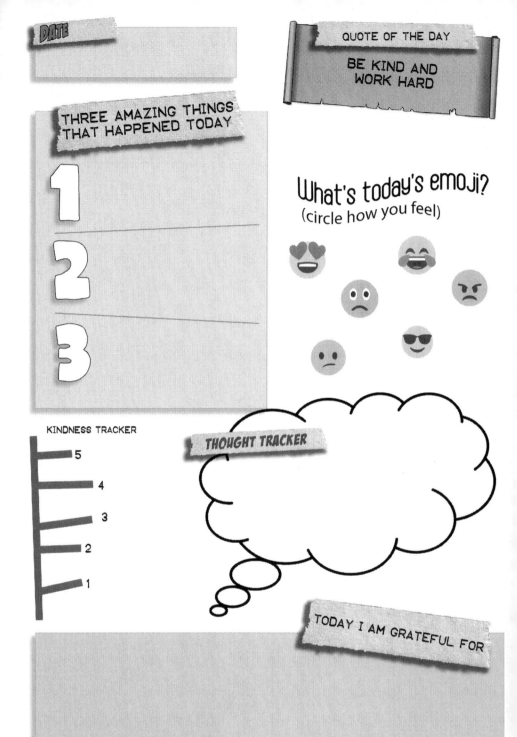

DATE

THREE AMAZING THINGS
THAT HAPPENED TODAY

1

2

3

What's today's emoji?
(circle how you feel)

KINDNESS TRACKER

5

4

3

2

1

THOUGHT TRACKER

TODAY I AM GRATEFUL FOR

THE GOOD THINGS CHECKLIST

- ☐ I TIDIED SOMETHING
- ☐ I WAS A GOOD FRIEND
- ☐ I SMILED ABOUT SOMETHING
- ☐ I HELPED SOMEONE
- ☐ I HELPED MYSELF
- ☐ I TRIED MY HARDEST

Daily Doodle OR Pattern

FEED THE WORRY MONSTER

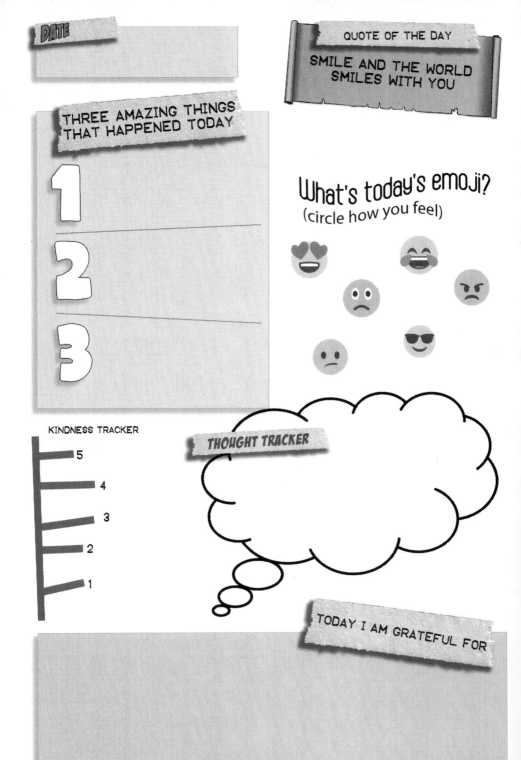

DATE

QUOTE OF THE DAY

SMILE AND THE WORLD
SMILES WITH YOU

THREE AMAZING THINGS
THAT HAPPENED TODAY

1

2

3

What's today's emoji?
(circle how you feel)

KINDNESS TRACKER

5
4
3
2
1

THOUGHT TRACKER

TODAY I AM GRATEFUL FOR

THE GOOD THINGS CHECKLIST

- ☐ I TIDIED SOMETHING
- ☐ I WAS A GOOD FRIEND
- ☐ I SMILED ABOUT SOMETHING
- ☐ I HELPED SOMEONE
- ☐ I HELPED MYSELF
- ☐ I TRIED MY HARDEST

Daily Doodle OR pattern

FEED THE WORRY MONSTER

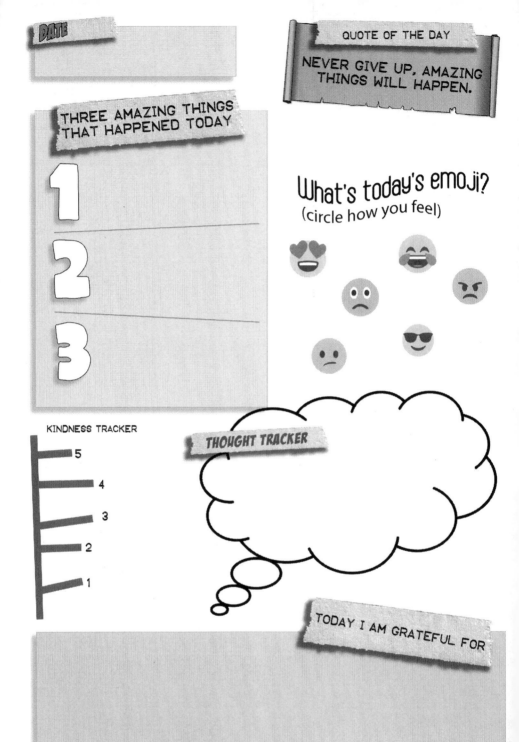

DATE

QUOTE OF THE DAY

NEVER GIVE UP, AMAZING THINGS WILL HAPPEN.

THREE AMAZING THINGS THAT HAPPENED TODAY

1

2

3

What's today's emoji?
(circle how you feel)

KINDNESS TRACKER

5

4

3

2

1

THOUGHT TRACKER

TODAY I AM GRATEFUL FOR

THE GOOD THINGS CHECKLIST

FEED THE WORRY MONSTER

- [ ] I TIDIED SOMETHING
- [ ] I WAS A GOOD FRIEND
- [ ] I SMILED ABOUT SOMETHING
- [ ] I HELPED SOMEONE
- [ ] I HELPED MYSELF
- [ ] I TRIED MY HARDEST

Daily Doodle OR Pattern

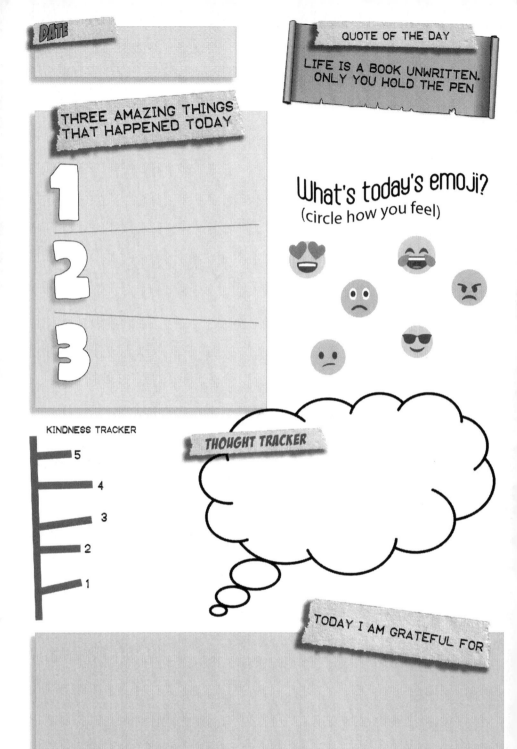

DATE

LIFE IS A BOOK UNWRITTEN.
ONLY YOU HOLD THE PEN

THREE AMAZING THINGS
THAT HAPPENED TODAY

1

2

3

What's today's emoji?
(circle how you feel)

KINDNESS TRACKER

5

4

3

2

1

THOUGHT TRACKER

TODAY I AM GRATEFUL FOR

THE GOOD THINGS
CHECKLIST

FEED THE WORRY MONSTER

- [ ] I TIDIED SOMETHING
- [ ] I WAS A GOOD FRIEND
- [ ] I SMILED ABOUT SOMETHING
- [ ] I HELPED SOMEONE
- [ ] I HELPED MYSELF
- [ ] I TRIED MY HARDEST

Daily Doodle OR Pattern

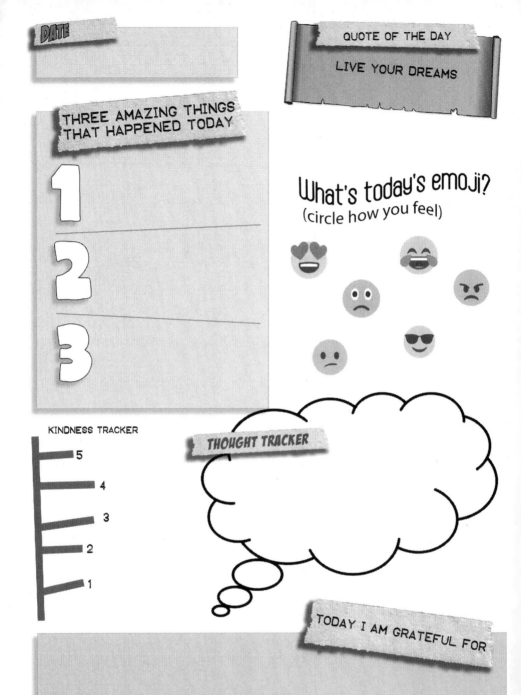

THE GOOD THINGS
CHECKLIST

FEED THE WORRY MONSTER

- ☐ I TIDIED SOMETHING
- ☐ I WAS A GOOD FRIEND
- ☐ I SMILED ABOUT SOMETHING
- ☐ I HELPED SOMEONE
- ☐ I HELPED MYSELF
- ☐ I TRIED MY HARDEST

Daily Doodle OR Pattern

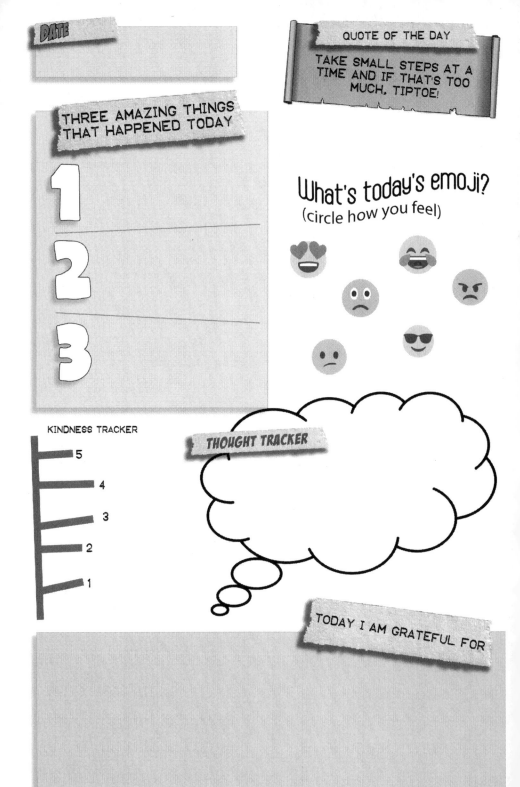

DATE

QUOTE OF THE DAY

TAKE SMALL STEPS AT A TIME AND IF THAT'S TOO MUCH, TIPTOE!

THREE AMAZING THINGS THAT HAPPENED TODAY

1
2
3

What's today's emoji?
(circle how you feel)

KINDNESS TRACKER

5
4
3
2
1

THOUGHT TRACKER

TODAY I AM GRATEFUL FOR

THE GOOD THINGS CHECKLIST

- ☐ I TIDIED SOMETHING
- ☐ I WAS A GOOD FRIEND
- ☐ I SMILED ABOUT SOMETHING
- ☐ I HELPED SOMEONE
- ☐ I HELPED MYSELF
- ☐ I TRIED MY HARDEST

FEED THE WORRY MONSTER

Daily Doodle or pattern

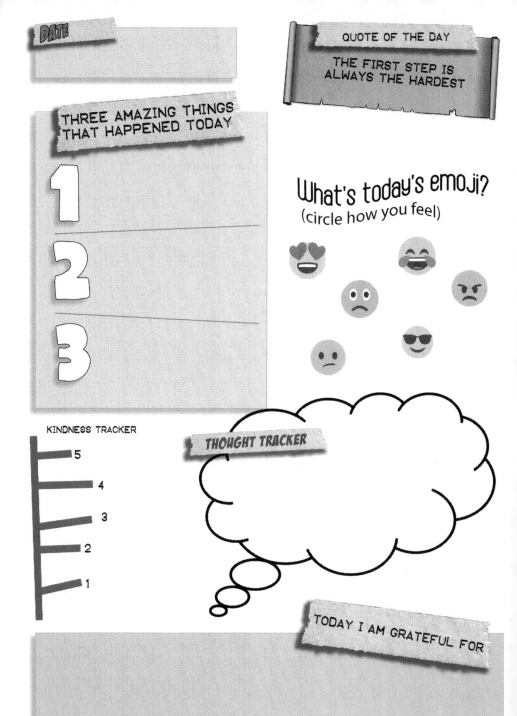

DATE

QUOTE OF THE DAY

THE FIRST STEP IS
ALWAYS THE HARDEST

THREE AMAZING THINGS
THAT HAPPENED TODAY

1

2

3

What's today's emoji?
(circle how you feel)

KINDNESS TRACKER

5

4

3

2

1

THOUGHT TRACKER

TODAY I AM GRATEFUL FOR

LISTS AND BULLET
JOURNAL DESIGNS

THE GOOD THINGS CHECKLIST

☐ I TIDIED SOMETHING

☐ I WAS A GOOD FRIEND

☐ I SMILED ABOUT SOMETHING

☐ I HELPED SOMEONE

☐ I HELPED MYSELF

☐ I TRIED MY HARDEST

Daily Doodle OR Pattern

FEED THE WORRY MONSTER

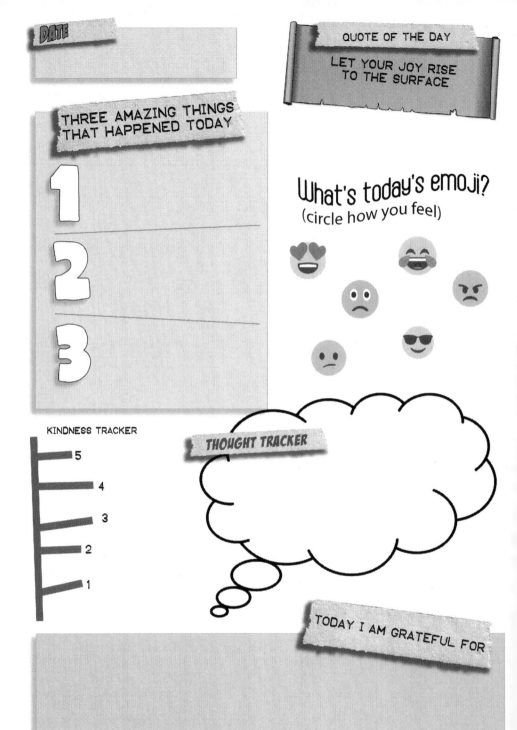

DATE

THREE AMAZING THINGS
THAT HAPPENED TODAY

1

2

3

What's today's emoji?
(circle how you feel)

KINDNESS TRACKER

5

4

3

2

1

THOUGHT TRACKER

TODAY I AM GRATEFUL FOR

THE GOOD THINGS CHECKLIST

FEED THE WORRY MONSTER

- ☐ I TIDIED SOMETHING
- ☐ I WAS A GOOD FRIEND
- ☐ I SMILED ABOUT SOMETHING
- ☐ I HELPED SOMEONE
- ☐ I HELPED MYSELF
- ☐ I TRIED MY HARDEST

Daily Doodle or Pattern

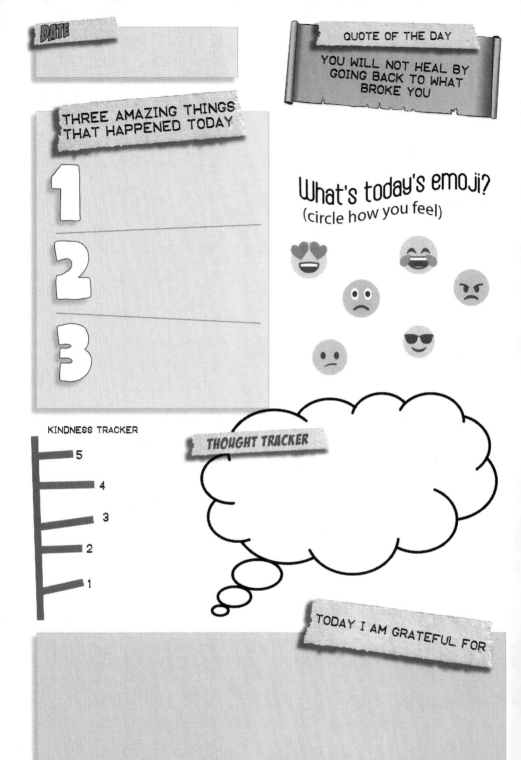

DATE

YOU WILL NOT HEAL BY GOING BACK TO WHAT BROKE YOU

THREE AMAZING THINGS THAT HAPPENED TODAY

1

2

3

What's today's emoji?
(circle how you feel)

KINDNESS TRACKER

5
4
3
2
1

THOUGHT TRACKER

TODAY I AM GRATEFUL FOR

THE GOOD THINGS
CHECKLIST

- [ ] I TIDIED SOMETHING
- [ ] I WAS A GOOD FRIEND
- [ ] I SMILED ABOUT SOMETHING
- [ ] I HELPED SOMEONE
- [ ] I HELPED MYSELF
- [ ] I TRIED MY HARDEST

Daily Doodle OR pattern

FEED THE WORRY MONSTER

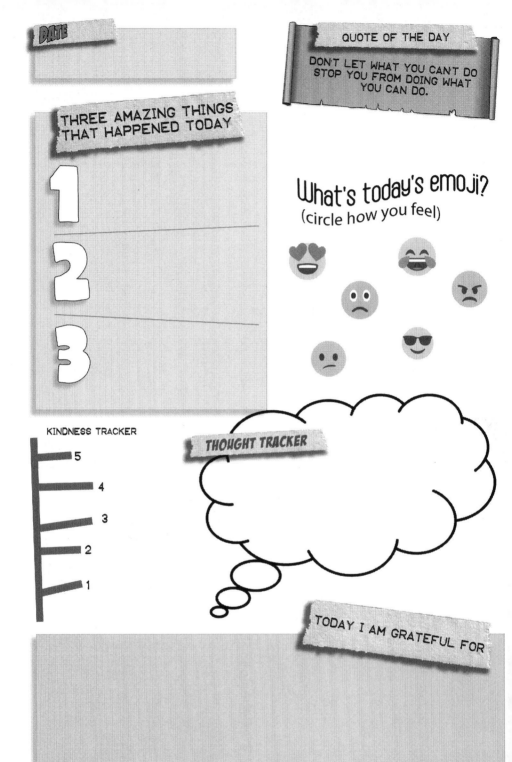

DATE

QUOTE OF THE DAY

DON'T LET WHAT YOU CAN'T DO STOP YOU FROM DOING WHAT YOU CAN DO.

THREE AMAZING THINGS THAT HAPPENED TODAY

1

2

3

What's today's emoji?
(circle how you feel)

KINDNESS TRACKER

5
4
3
2
1

THOUGHT TRACKER

TODAY I AM GRATEFUL FOR

LISTS AND BULLET
JOURNAL DESIGNS

THE GOOD THINGS CHECKLIST

- [ ] I TIDIED SOMETHING
- [ ] I WAS A GOOD FRIEND
- [ ] I SMILED ABOUT SOMETHING
- [ ] I HELPED SOMEONE
- [ ] I HELPED MYSELF
- [ ] I TRIED MY HARDEST

Daily Doodle OR Pattern

FEED THE WORRY MONSTER

DATE

THREE AMAZING THINGS
THAT HAPPENED TODAY

1

2

3

What's today's emoji?
(circle how you feel)

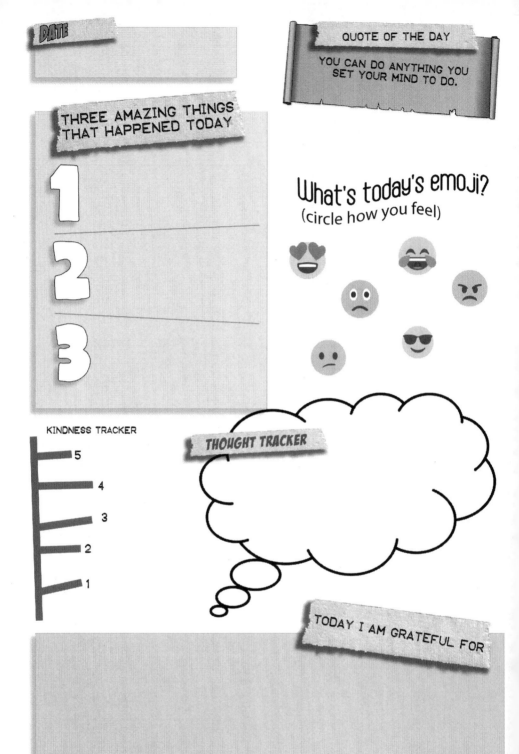

KINDNESS TRACKER

5

4

3

2

1

THOUGHT TRACKER

TODAY I AM GRATEFUL FOR

THE GOOD THINGS CHECKLIST

FEED THE WORRY MONSTER

- [ ] I TIDIED SOMETHING
- [ ] I WAS A GOOD FRIEND
- [ ] I SMILED ABOUT SOMETHING
- [ ] I HELPED SOMEONE
- [ ] I HELPED MYSELF
- [ ] I TRIED MY HARDEST

Daily Doodle OR Pattern

DATE

QUOTE OF THE DAY

YOU CAN'T DO IT... YET.

THREE AMAZING THINGS THAT HAPPENED TODAY

1

2

3

What's today's emoji?
(circle how you feel)

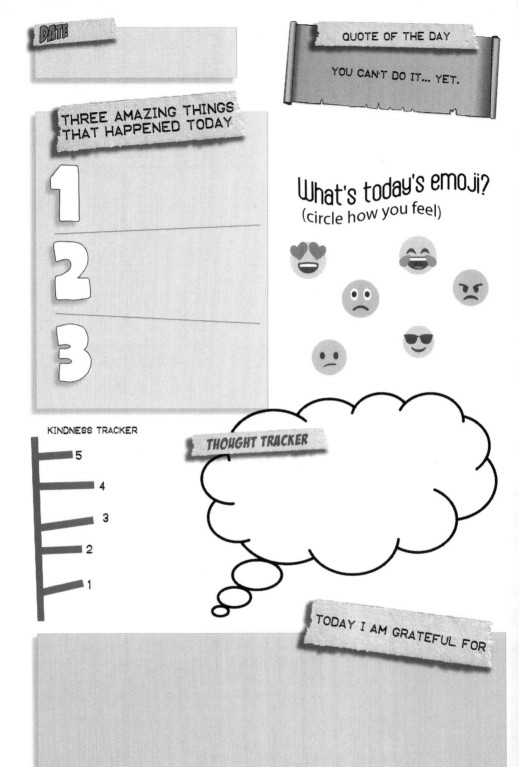

KINDNESS TRACKER

5

4

3

2

1

THOUGHT TRACKER

TODAY I AM GRATEFUL FOR

THE GOOD THINGS CHECKLIST

FEED THE WORRY MONSTER

- ☐ I TIDIED SOMETHING
- ☐ I WAS A GOOD FRIEND
- ☐ I SMILED ABOUT SOMETHING
- ☐ I HELPED SOMEONE
- ☐ I HELPED MYSELF
- ☐ I TRIED MY HARDEST

Daily Doodle or Pattern

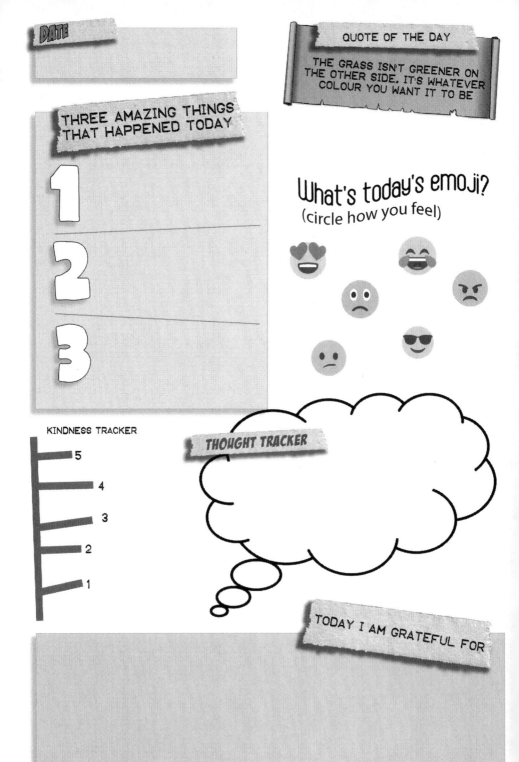

DATE

QUOTE OF THE DAY

THE GRASS ISN'T GREENER ON THE OTHER SIDE, IT'S WHATEVER COLOUR YOU WANT IT TO BE

THREE AMAZING THINGS THAT HAPPENED TODAY

1

2

3

What's today's emoji?
(circle how you feel)

KINDNESS TRACKER

5
4
3
2
1

THOUGHT TRACKER

TODAY I AM GRATEFUL FOR

THE GOOD THINGS CHECKLIST

- [ ] I TIDIED SOMETHING
- [ ] I WAS A GOOD FRIEND
- [ ] I SMILED ABOUT SOMETHING
- [ ] I HELPED SOMEONE
- [ ] I HELPED MYSELF
- [ ] I TRIED MY HARDEST

Daily Doodle OR pattern

FEED THE WORRY MONSTER

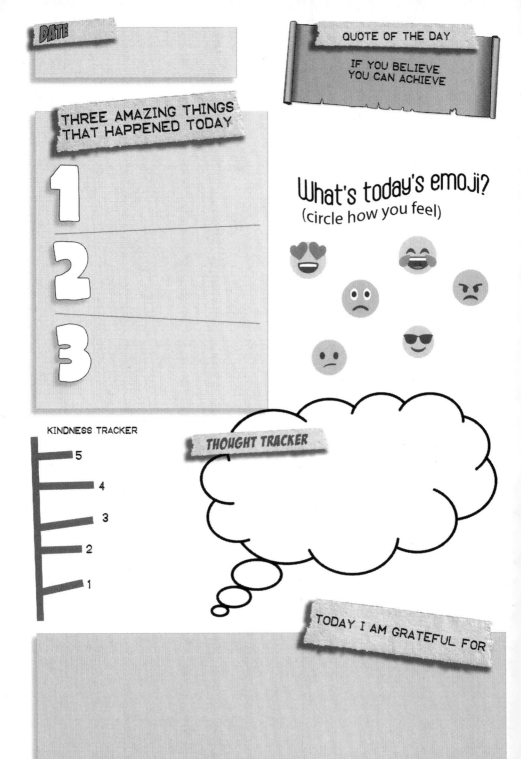

DATE

THREE AMAZING THINGS
THAT HAPPENED TODAY

1

2

3

What's today's emoji?
(circle how you feel)

KINDNESS TRACKER

5

4

3

2

1

THOUGHT TRACKER

TODAY I AM GRATEFUL FOR

LISTS AND BULLET JOURNAL DESIGNS

THE GOOD THINGS CHECKLIST

- ☐ I TIDIED SOMETHING
- ☐ I WAS A GOOD FRIEND
- ☐ I SMILED ABOUT SOMETHING
- ☐ I HELPED SOMEONE
- ☐ I HELPED MYSELF
- ☐ I TRIED MY HARDEST

Daily Doodle OR Pattern

 FEED THE WORRY MONSTER

DATE

THREE AMAZING THINGS
THAT HAPPENED TODAY

1

2

3

What's today's emoji?
(circle how you feel)

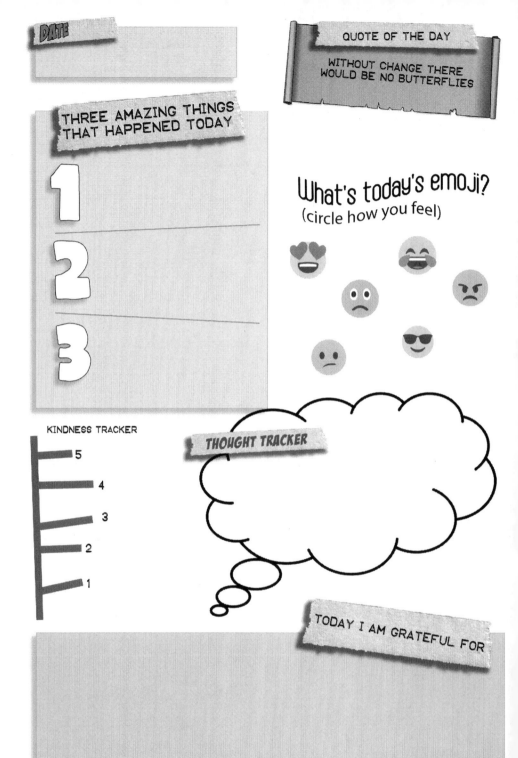

KINDNESS TRACKER

5
4
3
2
1

THOUGHT TRACKER

TODAY I AM GRATEFUL FOR

THE GOOD THINGS CHECKLIST

- [ ] I TIDIED SOMETHING
- [ ] I WAS A GOOD FRIEND
- [ ] I SMILED ABOUT SOMETHING
- [ ] I HELPED SOMEONE
- [ ] I HELPED MYSELF
- [ ] I TRIED MY HARDEST

Daily Doodle OR pattern

FEED THE WORRY MONSTER

DATE

THREE AMAZING THINGS THAT HAPPENED TODAY

1

2

3

What's today's emoji?
(circle how you feel)

KINDNESS TRACKER

5
4
3
2
1

THOUGHT TRACKER

TODAY I AM GRATEFUL FOR

THE GOOD THINGS CHECKLIST

- [ ] I TIDIED SOMETHING
- [ ] I WAS A GOOD FRIEND
- [ ] I SMILED ABOUT SOMETHING
- [ ] I HELPED SOMEONE
- [ ] I HELPED MYSELF
- [ ] I TRIED MY HARDEST

FEED THE WORRY MONSTER

Daily Doodle OR Pattern

DATE

QUOTE OF THE DAY

ONE DAY AT A TIME....

THREE AMAZING THINGS THAT HAPPENED TODAY

1

2

3

What's today's emoji?
(circle how you feel)

KINDNESS TRACKER

5

4

3

2

1

THOUGHT TRACKER

TODAY I AM GRATEFUL FOR

THE GOOD THINGS CHECKLIST

- [ ] I TIDIED SOMETHING
- [ ] I WAS A GOOD FRIEND
- [ ] I SMILED ABOUT SOMETHING
- [ ] I HELPED SOMEONE
- [ ] I HELPED MYSELF
- [ ] I TRIED MY HARDEST

FEED THE WORRY MONSTER

Daily Doodle OR pattern

DATE

QUOTE OF THE DAY

EVERYTHING NEW TAKES
TIME TO LEARN.

THREE AMAZING THINGS
THAT HAPPENED TODAY

1

2

3

What's today's emoji?
(circle how you feel)

KINDNESS TRACKER

5

4

3

2

1

THOUGHT TRACKER

TODAY I AM GRATEFUL FOR

THE GOOD THINGS CHECKLIST

- ☐ I TIDIED SOMETHING
- ☐ I WAS A GOOD FRIEND
- ☐ I SMILED ABOUT SOMETHING
- ☐ I HELPED SOMEONE
- ☐ I HELPED MYSELF
- ☐ I TRIED MY HARDEST

FEED THE WORRY MONSTER

Daily Doodle OR pattern

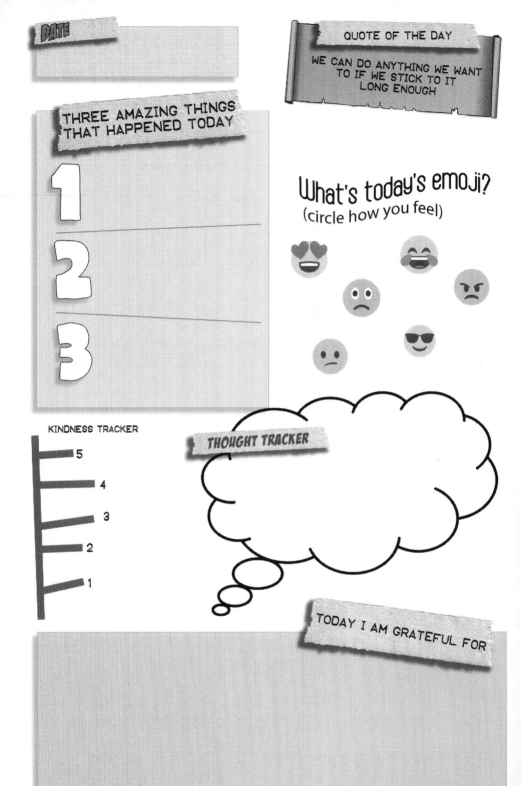

DATE

QUOTE OF THE DAY

WE CAN DO ANYTHING WE WANT TO IF WE STICK TO IT LONG ENOUGH

THREE AMAZING THINGS THAT HAPPENED TODAY

1

2

3

What's today's emoji?
(circle how you feel)

KINDNESS TRACKER

5

4

3

2

1

THOUGHT TRACKER

TODAY I AM GRATEFUL FOR

THE GOOD THINGS
CHECKLIST

☐ I TIDIED SOMETHING

☐ I WAS A GOOD FRIEND

☐ I SMILED ABOUT SOMETHING

☐ I HELPED SOMEONE

☐ I HELPED MYSELF

☐ I TRIED MY HARDEST

FEED THE WORRY MONSTER

Daily Doodle or Pattern

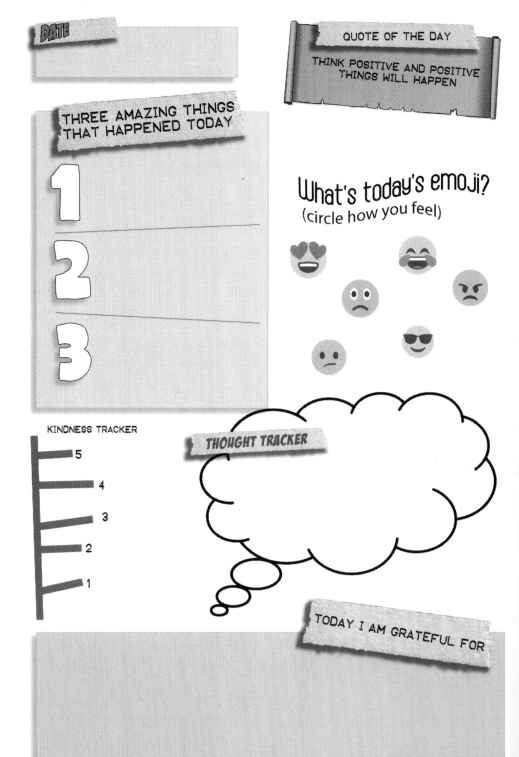

DATE

QUOTE OF THE DAY

THINK POSITIVE AND POSITIVE THINGS WILL HAPPEN

THREE AMAZING THINGS THAT HAPPENED TODAY

1

2

3

What's today's emoji?
(circle how you feel)

KINDNESS TRACKER

5
4
3
2
1

THOUGHT TRACKER

TODAY I AM GRATEFUL FOR

THE GOOD THINGS CHECKLIST

FEED THE WORRY MONSTER

- ☐ I TIDIED SOMETHING
- ☐ I WAS A GOOD FRIEND
- ☐ I SMILED ABOUT SOMETHING
- ☐ I HELPED SOMEONE
- ☐ I HELPED MYSELF
- ☐ I TRIED MY HARDEST

Daily Doodle or Pattern

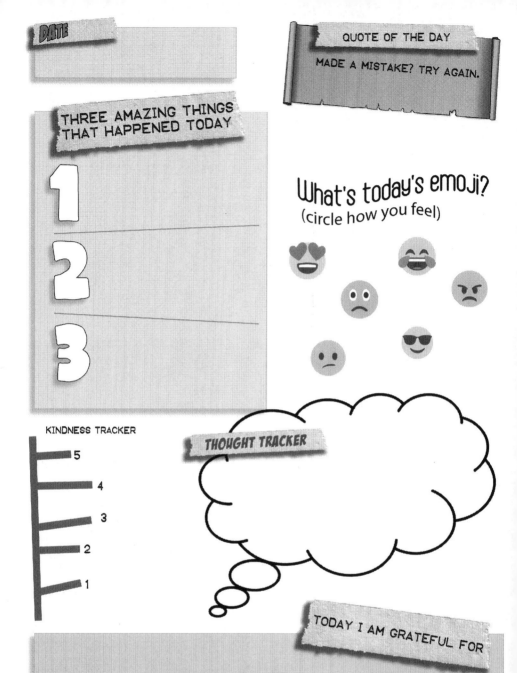

DATE

QUOTE OF THE DAY

MADE A MISTAKE? TRY AGAIN.

THREE AMAZING THINGS THAT HAPPENED TODAY

1

2

3

What's today's emoji?
(circle how you feel)

KINDNESS TRACKER

5
4
3
2
1

THOUGHT TRACKER

TODAY I AM GRATEFUL FOR

THE GOOD THINGS CHECKLIST

- ☐ I TIDIED SOMETHING
- ☐ I WAS A GOOD FRIEND
- ☐ I SMILED ABOUT SOMETHING
- ☐ I HELPED SOMEONE
- ☐ I HELPED MYSELF
- ☐ I TRIED MY HARDEST

Daily Doodle OR Pattern

FEED THE WORRY MONSTER

DATE

THREE AMAZING THINGS
THAT HAPPENED TODAY

1

2

3

What's today's emoji?
(circle how you feel)

KINDNESS TRACKER

5

4

3

2

1

THOUGHT TRACKER

TODAY I AM GRATEFUL FOR

THE GOOD THINGS CHECKLIST

☐ I TIDIED SOMETHING

☐ I WAS A GOOD FRIEND

☐ I SMILED ABOUT SOMETHING

☐ I HELPED SOMEONE

☐ I HELPED MYSELF

☐ I TRIED MY HARDEST

FEED THE WORRY MONSTER

Daily Doodle or pattern

DATE

QUOTE OF THE DAY

IF PLAN A DOESN'T WORK THERE ARE 25 MORE LETTERS.

THREE AMAZING THINGS THAT HAPPENED TODAY

1

2

3

What's today's emoji?
(circle how you feel)

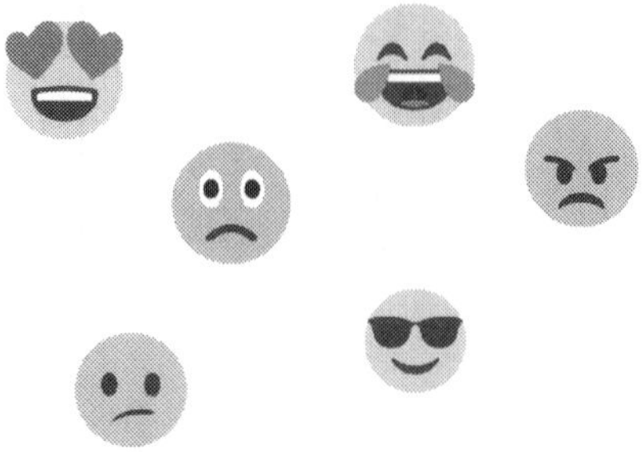

KINDNESS TRACKER

5

4

3

2

1

THOUGHT TRACKER

TODAY I AM GRATEFUL FOR

THE GOOD THINGS CHECKLIST

FEED THE WORRY MONSTER

- [ ] I TIDIED SOMETHING
- [ ] I WAS A GOOD FRIEND
- [ ] I SMILED ABOUT SOMETHING
- [ ] I HELPED SOMEONE
- [ ] I HELPED MYSELF
- [ ] I TRIED MY HARDEST

Daily Doodle or Pattern

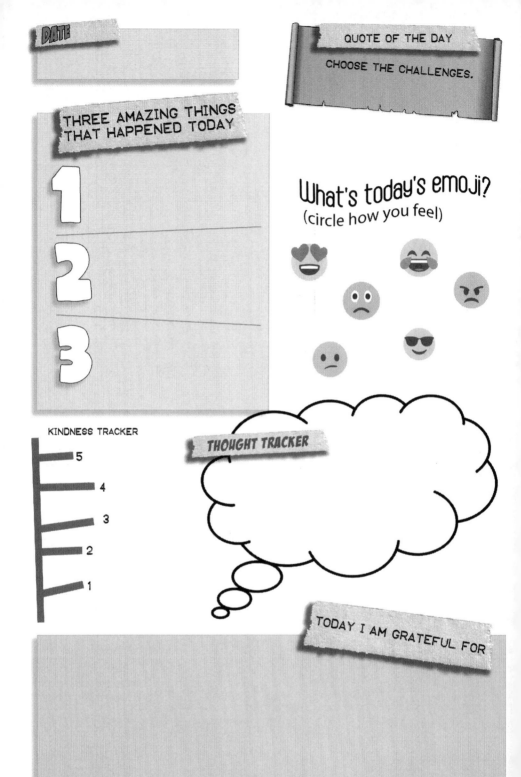

DATE

QUOTE OF THE DAY

CHOOSE THE CHALLENGES.

THREE AMAZING THINGS THAT HAPPENED TODAY

1

2

3

What's today's emoji?
(circle how you feel)

KINDNESS TRACKER

5
4
3
2
1

THOUGHT TRACKER

TODAY I AM GRATEFUL FOR

THE GOOD THINGS CHECKLIST

- ☐ I TIDIED SOMETHING
- ☐ I WAS A GOOD FRIEND
- ☐ I SMILED ABOUT SOMETHING
- ☐ I HELPED SOMEONE
- ☐ I HELPED MYSELF
- ☐ I TRIED MY HARDEST

Daily Doodle OR Pattern

FEED THE WORRY MONSTER

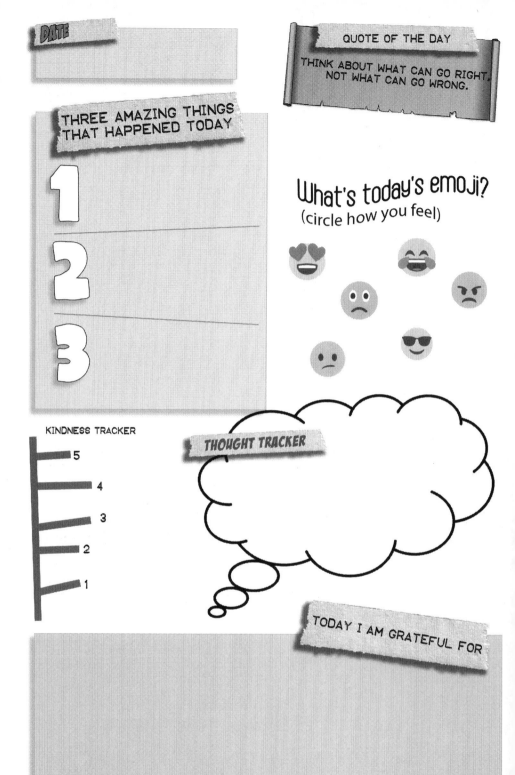

THE GOOD THINGS CHECKLIST

- [ ] I TIDIED SOMETHING
- [ ] I WAS A GOOD FRIEND
- [ ] I SMILED ABOUT SOMETHING
- [ ] I HELPED SOMEONE
- [ ] I HELPED MYSELF
- [ ] I TRIED MY HARDEST

Daily Doodle OR Pattern

FEED THE WORRY MONSTER

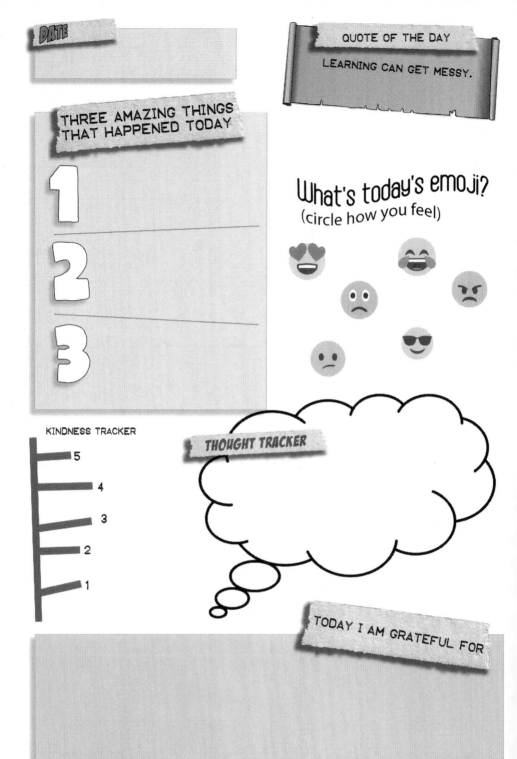

DATE

QUOTE OF THE DAY

LEARNING CAN GET MESSY.

THREE AMAZING THINGS THAT HAPPENED TODAY

1

2

3

What's today's emoji?
(circle how you feel)

KINDNESS TRACKER

5

4

3

2

1

THOUGHT TRACKER

TODAY I AM GRATEFUL FOR

THE GOOD THINGS
CHECKLIST

- ☐ I TIDIED SOMETHING
- ☐ I WAS A GOOD FRIEND
- ☐ I SMILED ABOUT SOMETHING
- ☐ I HELPED SOMEONE
- ☐ I HELPED MYSELF
- ☐ I TRIED MY HARDEST

Daily Doodle OR Pattern

FEED THE WORRY MONSTER

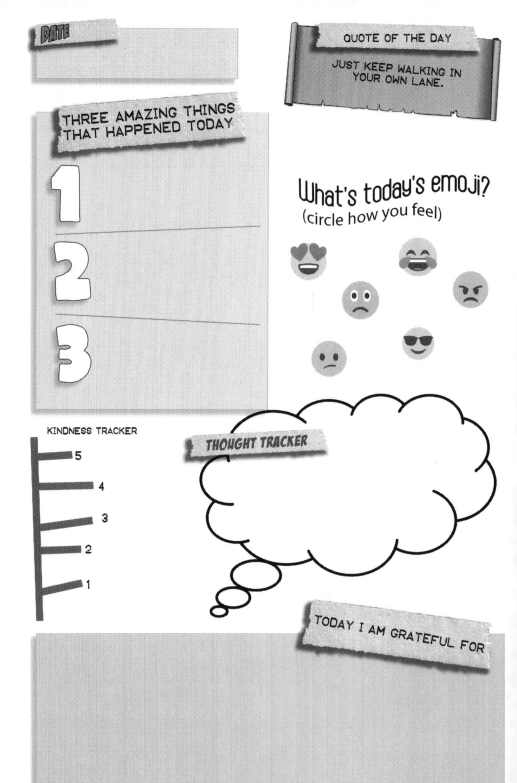

DATE

QUOTE OF THE DAY

JUST KEEP WALKING IN YOUR OWN LANE.

THREE AMAZING THINGS THAT HAPPENED TODAY

1

2

3

What's today's emoji?
(circle how you feel)

KINDNESS TRACKER

5

4

3

2

1

THOUGHT TRACKER

TODAY I AM GRATEFUL FOR

THE GOOD THINGS CHECKLIST

- ☐ I TIDIED SOMETHING
- ☐ I WAS A GOOD FRIEND
- ☐ I SMILED ABOUT SOMETHING
- ☐ I HELPED SOMEONE
- ☐ I HELPED MYSELF
- ☐ I TRIED MY HARDEST

FEED THE WORRY MONSTER

Daily Doodle or Pattern

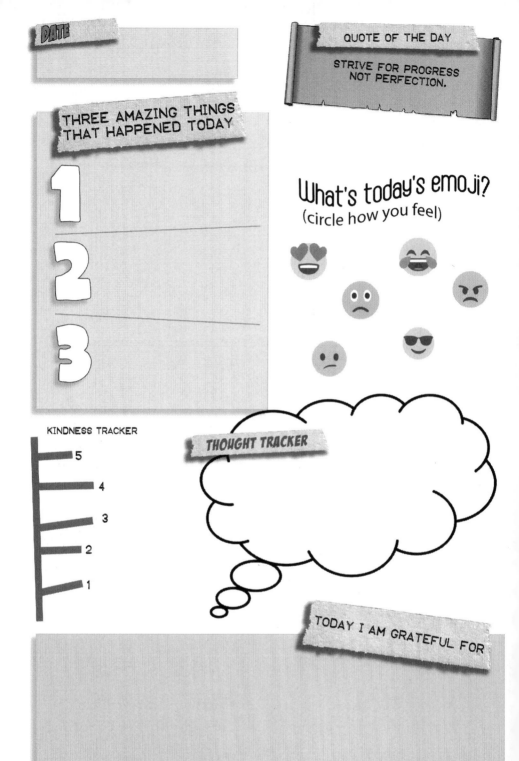

DATE

QUOTE OF THE DAY

STRIVE FOR PROGRESS
NOT PERFECTION.

THREE AMAZING THINGS
THAT HAPPENED TODAY

1

2

3

What's today's emoji?
(circle how you feel)

KINDNESS TRACKER

5
4
3
2
1

THOUGHT TRACKER

TODAY I AM GRATEFUL FOR

THE GOOD THINGS CHECKLIST

FEED THE WORRY MONSTER

- [ ] I TIDIED SOMETHING
- [ ] I WAS A GOOD FRIEND
- [ ] I SMILED ABOUT SOMETHING
- [ ] I HELPED SOMEONE
- [ ] I HELPED MYSELF
- [ ] I TRIED MY HARDEST

Daily Doodle or pattern

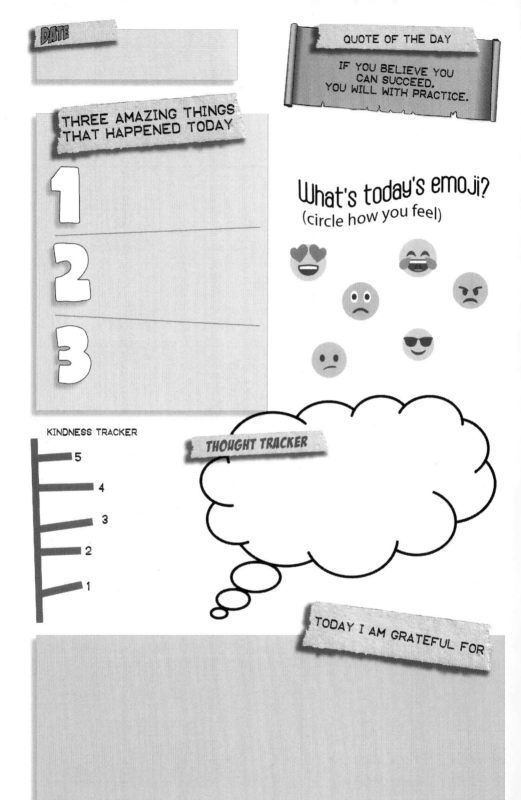

DATE

QUOTE OF THE DAY

IF YOU BELIEVE YOU
CAN SUCCEED,
YOU WILL WITH PRACTICE.

THREE AMAZING THINGS
THAT HAPPENED TODAY

1

2

3

What's today's emoji?
(circle how you feel)

KINDNESS TRACKER

5

4

3

2

1

THOUGHT TRACKER

TODAY I AM GRATEFUL FOR

THE GOOD THINGS CHECKLIST

- ☐ I TIDIED SOMETHING
- ☐ I WAS A GOOD FRIEND
- ☐ I SMILED ABOUT SOMETHING
- ☐ I HELPED SOMEONE
- ☐ I HELPED MYSELF
- ☐ I TRIED MY HARDEST

FEED THE WORRY MONSTER

Daily Doodle or Pattern

QUOTE OF THE DAY

MISTAKES ARE PROOF
THAT YOU ARE TRYING.

THREE AMAZING THINGS
THAT HAPPENED TODAY

1

2

3

What's today's emoji?
(circle how you feel)

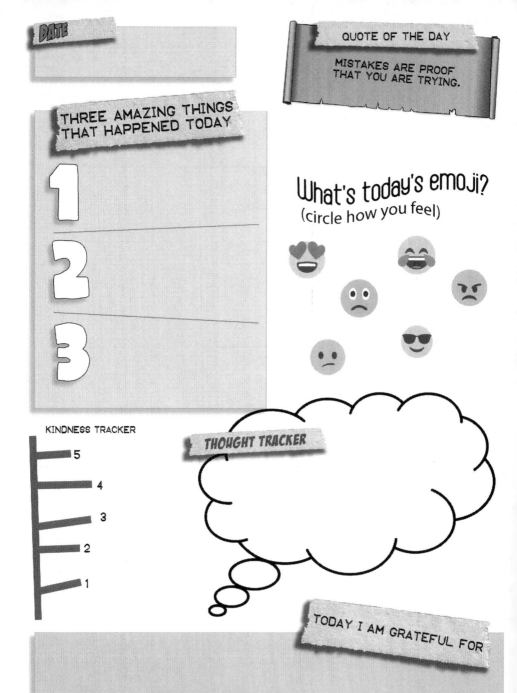

KINDNESS TRACKER

5

4

3

2

1

THOUGHT TRACKER

TODAY I AM GRATEFUL FOR

THE GOOD THINGS CHECKLIST

FEED THE WORRY MONSTER

- ☐ I TIDIED SOMETHING
- ☐ I WAS A GOOD FRIEND
- ☐ I SMILED ABOUT SOMETHING
- ☐ I HELPED SOMEONE
- ☐ I HELPED MYSELF
- ☐ I TRIED MY HARDEST

Daily Doodle OR Pattern

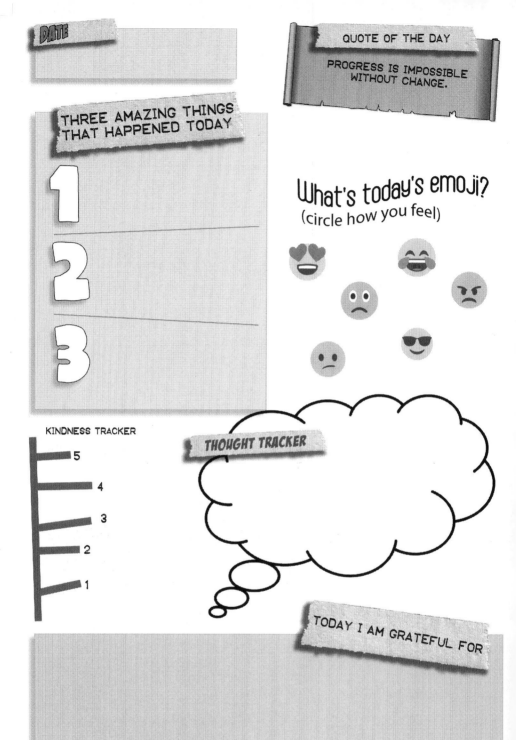

DATE

QUOTE OF THE DAY

PROGRESS IS IMPOSSIBLE WITHOUT CHANGE.

THREE AMAZING THINGS THAT HAPPENED TODAY

1
2
3

What's today's emoji?
(circle how you feel)

KINDNESS TRACKER

5
4
3
2
1

THOUGHT TRACKER

TODAY I AM GRATEFUL FOR

THE GOOD THINGS CHECKLIST

- ☐ I TIDIED SOMETHING
- ☐ I WAS A GOOD FRIEND
- ☐ I SMILED ABOUT SOMETHING
- ☐ I HELPED SOMEONE
- ☐ I HELPED MYSELF
- ☐ I TRIED MY HARDEST

Daily Doodle or Pattern

FEED THE WORRY MONSTER

DATE

THREE AMAZING THINGS
THAT HAPPENED TODAY

1

2

3

What's today's emoji?
(circle how you feel)

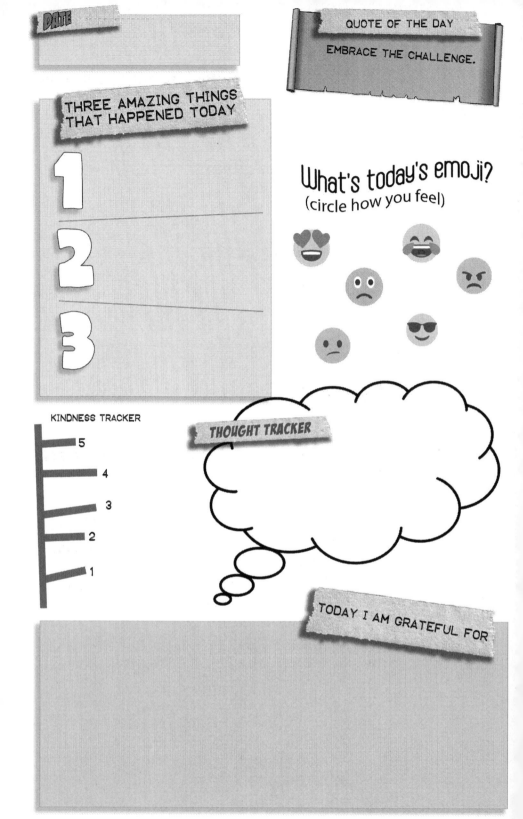

KINDNESS TRACKER

5
4
3
2
1

THOUGHT TRACKER

TODAY I AM GRATEFUL FOR

THE GOOD THINGS CHECKLIST

FEED THE WORRY MONSTER

- [ ] I TIDIED SOMETHING
- [ ] I WAS A GOOD FRIEND
- [ ] I SMILED ABOUT SOMETHING
- [ ] I HELPED SOMEONE
- [ ] I HELPED MYSELF
- [ ] I TRIED MY HARDEST

Daily Doodle or pattern

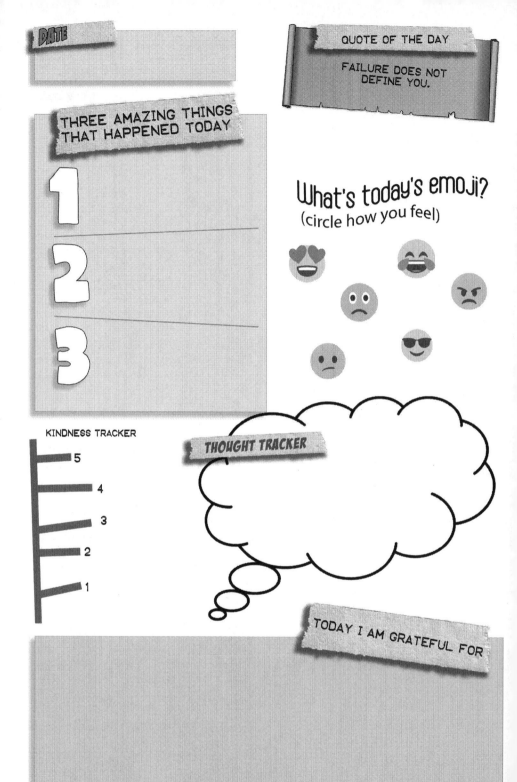

THE GOOD THINGS CHECKLIST

- [ ] I TIDIED SOMETHING
- [ ] I WAS A GOOD FRIEND
- [ ] I SMILED ABOUT SOMETHING
- [ ] I HELPED SOMEONE
- [ ] I HELPED MYSELF
- [ ] I TRIED MY HARDEST

FEED THE WORRY MONSTER

Daily Doodle OR pattern

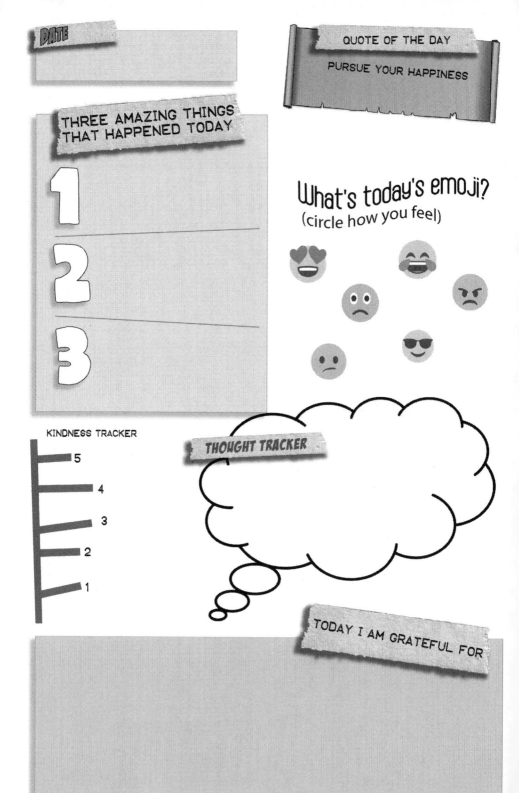

DATE

QUOTE OF THE DAY

PURSUE YOUR HAPPINESS

THREE AMAZING THINGS THAT HAPPENED TODAY

1

2

3

What's today's emoji?
(circle how you feel)

KINDNESS TRACKER

5
4
3
2
1

THOUGHT TRACKER

TODAY I AM GRATEFUL FOR

THE GOOD THINGS CHECKLIST

☐ I TIDIED SOMETHING

☐ I WAS A GOOD FRIEND

☐ I SMILED ABOUT SOMETHING

☐ I HELPED SOMEONE

☐ I HELPED MYSELF

☐ I TRIED MY HARDEST

FEED THE WORRY MONSTER

Daily Doodle OR Pattern

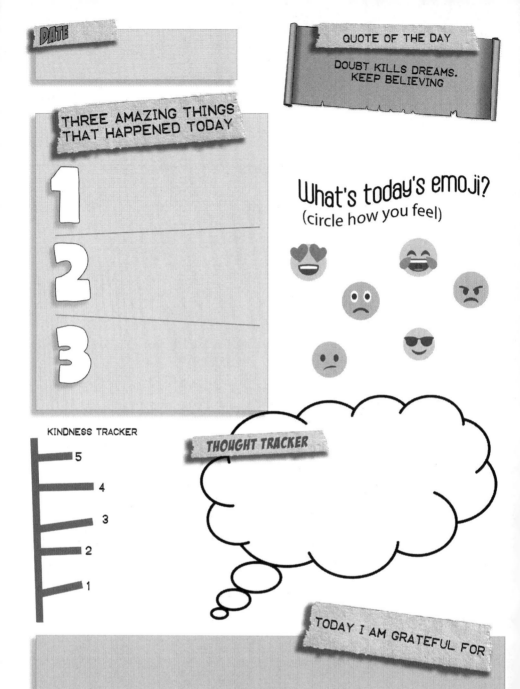

DATE

QUOTE OF THE DAY

DOUBT KILLS DREAMS. KEEP BELIEVING

THREE AMAZING THINGS THAT HAPPENED TODAY

1

2

3

What's today's emoji?
(circle how you feel)

KINDNESS TRACKER

5
4
3
2
1

THOUGHT TRACKER

TODAY I AM GRATEFUL FOR

THE GOOD THINGS CHECKLIST

- ☐ I TIDIED SOMETHING
- ☐ I WAS A GOOD FRIEND
- ☐ I SMILED ABOUT SOMETHING
- ☐ I HELPED SOMEONE
- ☐ I HELPED MYSELF
- ☐ I TRIED MY HARDEST

Daily Doodle OR Pattern

FEED THE WORRY MONSTER

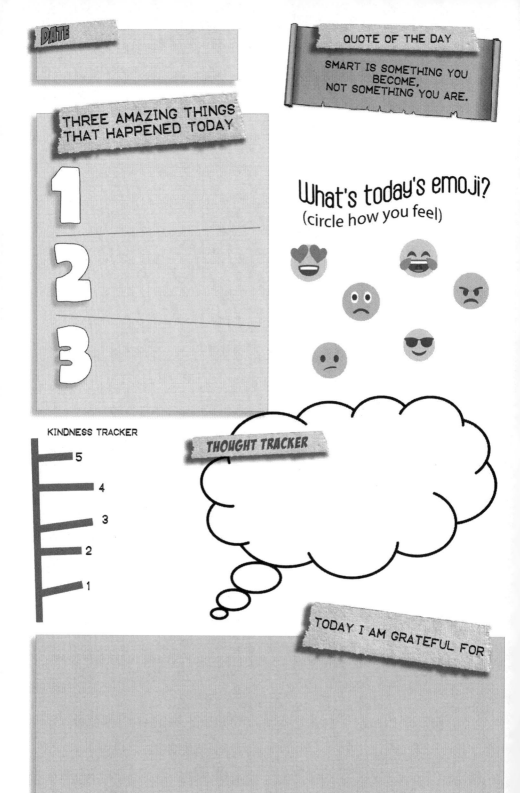

DATE

QUOTE OF THE DAY

SMART IS SOMETHING YOU BECOME,
NOT SOMETHING YOU ARE.

THREE AMAZING THINGS THAT HAPPENED TODAY

1

2

3

What's today's emoji?
(circle how you feel)

KINDNESS TRACKER

5
4
3
2
1

THOUGHT TRACKER

TODAY I AM GRATEFUL FOR

THE GOOD THINGS CHECKLIST

- [ ] I TIDIED SOMETHING
- [ ] I WAS A GOOD FRIEND
- [ ] I SMILED ABOUT SOMETHING
- [ ] I HELPED SOMEONE
- [ ] I HELPED MYSELF
- [ ] I TRIED MY HARDEST

Daily Doodle OR pattern

FEED THE WORRY MONSTER

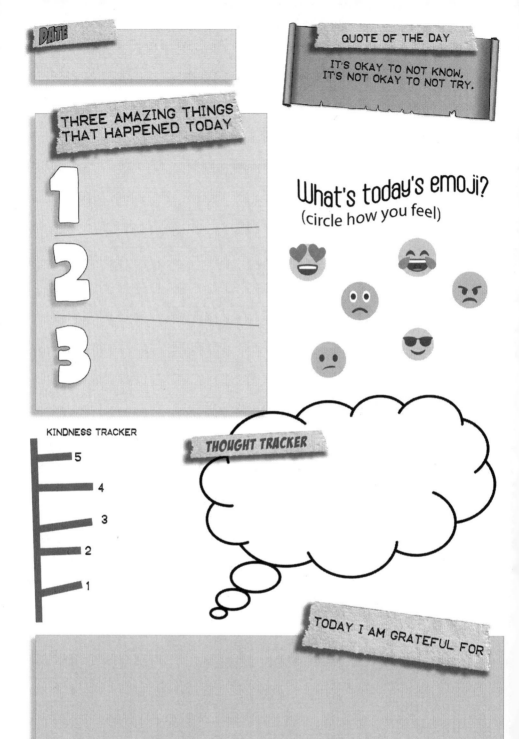

DATE

QUOTE OF THE DAY

IT'S OKAY TO NOT KNOW,
IT'S NOT OKAY TO NOT TRY.

THREE AMAZING THINGS
THAT HAPPENED TODAY

1

2

3

What's today's emoji?
(circle how you feel)

KINDNESS TRACKER

5

4

3

2

1

THOUGHT TRACKER

TODAY I AM GRATEFUL FOR

LISTS AND BULLET JOURNAL DESIGNS

THE GOOD THINGS CHECKLIST

☐ I TIDIED SOMETHING

☐ I WAS A GOOD FRIEND

☐ I SMILED ABOUT SOMETHING

☐ I HELPED SOMEONE

☐ I HELPED MYSELF

☐ I TRIED MY HARDEST

Daily Doodle or Pattern

FEED THE WORRY MONSTER

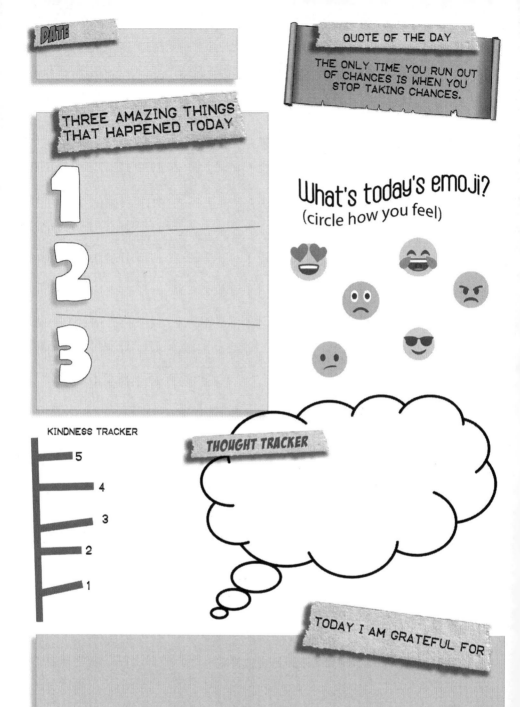

DATE

QUOTE OF THE DAY

THE ONLY TIME YOU RUN OUT OF CHANCES IS WHEN YOU STOP TAKING CHANCES.

THREE AMAZING THINGS THAT HAPPENED TODAY

1
2
3

What's today's emoji?
(circle how you feel)

KINDNESS TRACKER

5
4
3
2
1

THOUGHT TRACKER

TODAY I AM GRATEFUL FOR

THE GOOD THINGS CHECKLIST

- ☐ I TIDIED SOMETHING
- ☐ I WAS A GOOD FRIEND
- ☐ I SMILED ABOUT SOMETHING
- ☐ I HELPED SOMEONE
- ☐ I HELPED MYSELF
- ☐ I TRIED MY HARDEST

FEED THE WORRY MONSTER

Daily Doodle or Pattern

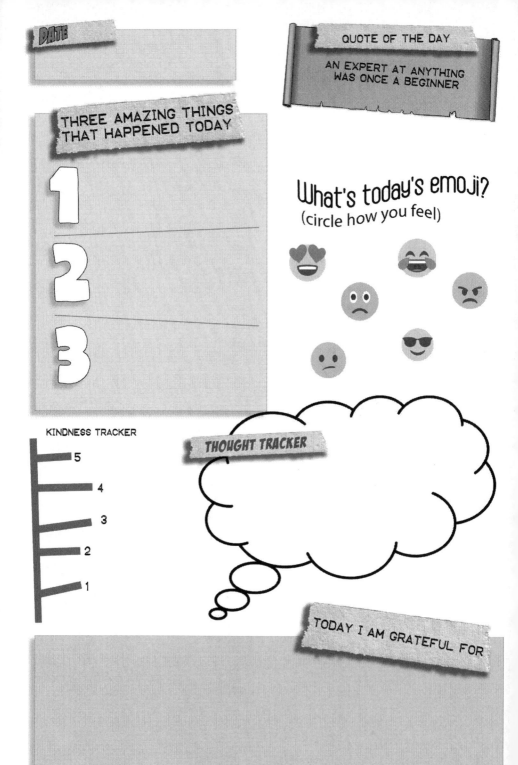

THE GOOD THINGS CHECKLIST

- ☐ I TIDIED SOMETHING
- ☐ I WAS A GOOD FRIEND
- ☐ I SMILED ABOUT SOMETHING
- ☐ I HELPED SOMEONE
- ☐ I HELPED MYSELF
- ☐ I TRIED MY HARDEST

Daily Doodle OR pattern

FEED THE WORRY MONSTER

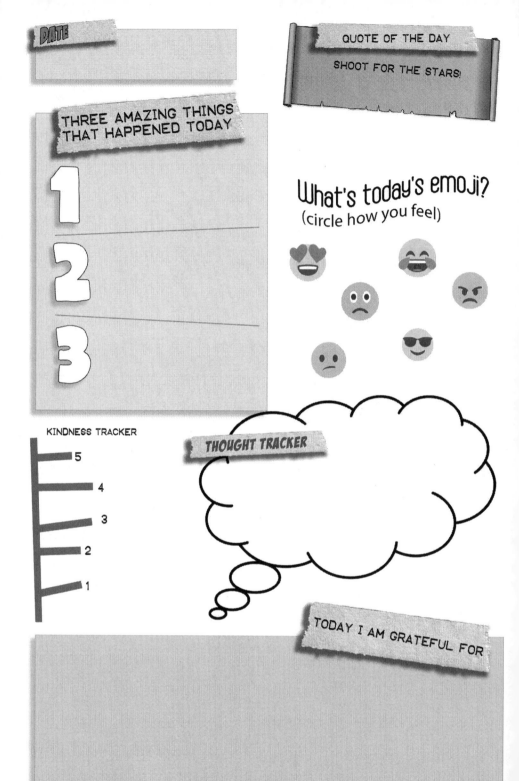

DATE

QUOTE OF THE DAY

SHOOT FOR THE STARS!

THREE AMAZING THINGS THAT HAPPENED TODAY

1

2

3

What's today's emoji?
(circle how you feel)

KINDNESS TRACKER

5
4
3
2
1

THOUGHT TRACKER

TODAY I AM GRATEFUL FOR

THE GOOD THINGS CHECKLIST

- [ ] I TIDIED SOMETHING
- [ ] I WAS A GOOD FRIEND
- [ ] I SMILED ABOUT SOMETHING
- [ ] I HELPED SOMEONE
- [ ] I HELPED MYSELF
- [ ] I TRIED MY HARDEST

Daily Doodle or pattern

FEED THE WORRY MONSTER

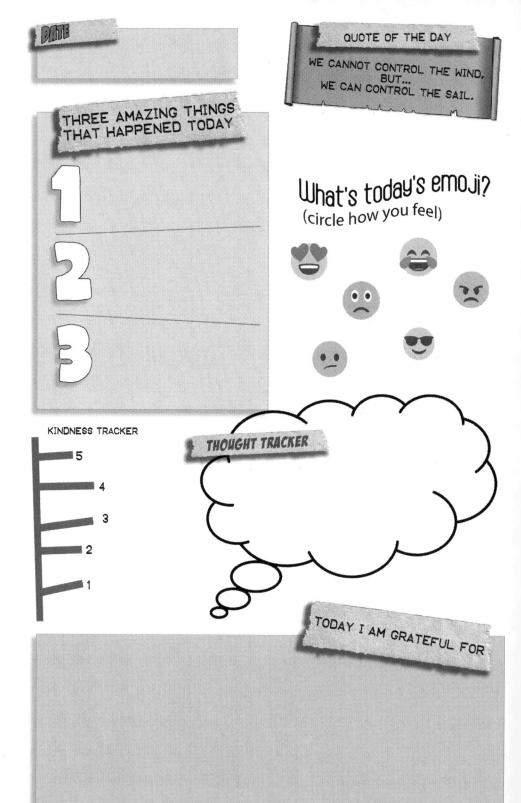

DATE

THREE AMAZING THINGS
THAT HAPPENED TODAY

1

2

3

What's today's emoji?
(circle how you feel)

KINDNESS TRACKER

5

4

3

2

1

THOUGHT TRACKER

TODAY I AM GRATEFUL FOR

THE GOOD THINGS CHECKLIST

- [ ] I TIDIED SOMETHING
- [ ] I WAS A GOOD FRIEND
- [ ] I SMILED ABOUT SOMETHING
- [ ] I HELPED SOMEONE
- [ ] I HELPED MYSELF
- [ ] I TRIED MY HARDEST

Daily Doodle OR Pattern

FEED THE WORRY MONSTER

QUOTE OF THE DAY

MISTAKES MAKE A DIFFERENCE

THREE AMAZING THINGS
THAT HAPPENED TODAY

1

2

3

What's today's emoji?
(circle how you feel)

KINDNESS TRACKER

5
4
3
2
1

THOUGHT TRACKER

TODAY I AM GRATEFUL FOR

THE GOOD THINGS CHECKLIST

- [ ] I TIDIED SOMETHING
- [ ] I WAS A GOOD FRIEND
- [ ] I SMILED ABOUT SOMETHING
- [ ] I HELPED SOMEONE
- [ ] I HELPED MYSELF
- [ ] I TRIED MY HARDEST

Daily Doodle OR pattern

FEED THE WORRY MONSTER

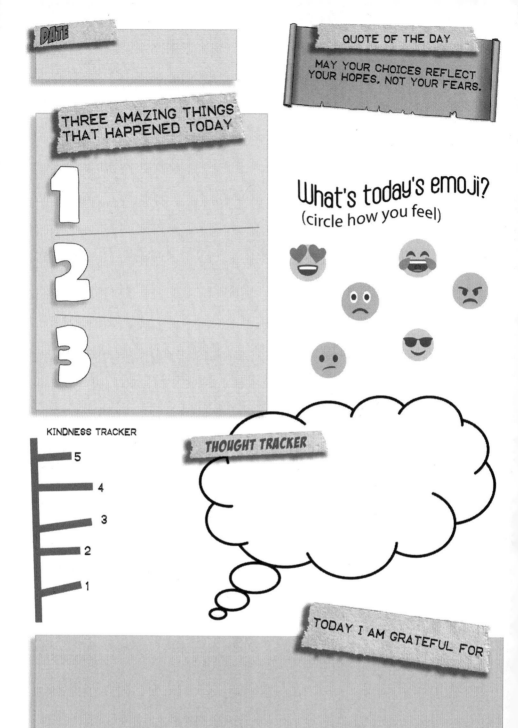

DATE

THREE AMAZING THINGS
THAT HAPPENED TODAY

1

2

3

QUOTE OF THE DAY

MAY YOUR CHOICES REFLECT
YOUR HOPES, NOT YOUR FEARS.

What's today's emoji?
(circle how you feel)

KINDNESS TRACKER

5

4

3

2

1

THOUGHT TRACKER

TODAY I AM GRATEFUL FOR

THE GOOD THINGS CHECKLIST

FEED THE WORRY MONSTER

- ☐ I TIDIED SOMETHING
- ☐ I WAS A GOOD FRIEND
- ☐ I SMILED ABOUT SOMETHING
- ☐ I HELPED SOMEONE
- ☐ I HELPED MYSELF
- ☐ I TRIED MY HARDEST

Daily Doodle or Pattern

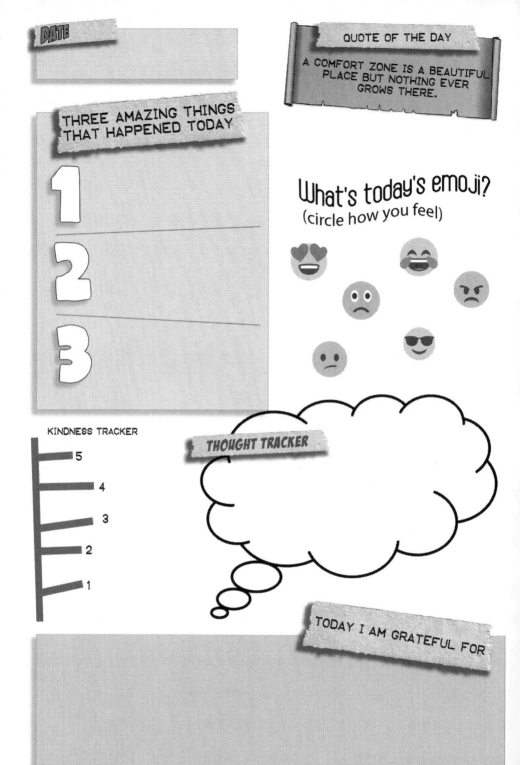

DATE

QUOTE OF THE DAY

A COMFORT ZONE IS A BEAUTIFUL PLACE BUT NOTHING EVER GROWS THERE.

THREE AMAZING THINGS THAT HAPPENED TODAY

1
2
3

What's today's emoji?
(circle how you feel)

KINDNESS TRACKER

5
4
3
2
1

THOUGHT TRACKER

TODAY I AM GRATEFUL FOR

THE GOOD THINGS CHECKLIST

- ☐ I TIDIED SOMETHING
- ☐ I WAS A GOOD FRIEND
- ☐ I SMILED ABOUT SOMETHING
- ☐ I HELPED SOMEONE
- ☐ I HELPED MYSELF
- ☐ I TRIED MY HARDEST

FEED THE WORRY MONSTER

Daily Doodle OR Pattern

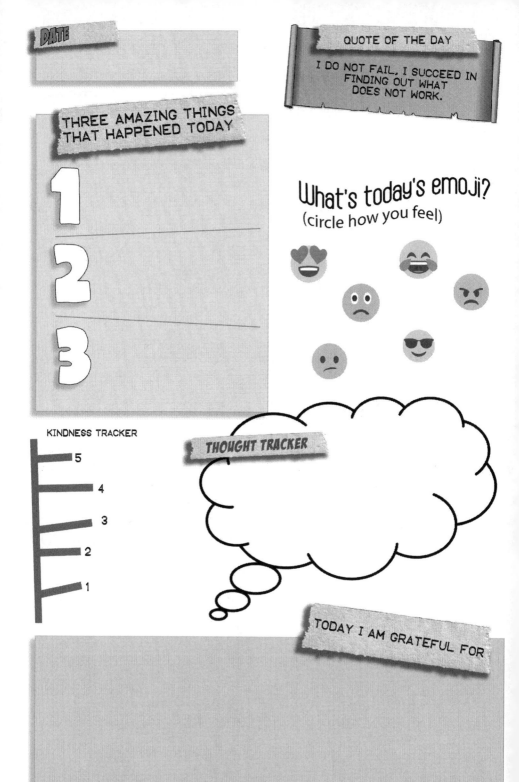

DATE

QUOTE OF THE DAY

I DO NOT FAIL, I SUCCEED IN FINDING OUT WHAT DOES NOT WORK.

THREE AMAZING THINGS THAT HAPPENED TODAY

1

2

3

What's today's emoji?
(circle how you feel)

KINDNESS TRACKER

5
4
3
2
1

THOUGHT TRACKER

TODAY I AM GRATEFUL FOR

THE GOOD THINGS CHECKLIST

- [ ] I TIDIED SOMETHING
- [ ] I WAS A GOOD FRIEND
- [ ] I SMILED ABOUT SOMETHING
- [ ] I HELPED SOMEONE
- [ ] I HELPED MYSELF
- [ ] I TRIED MY HARDEST

FEED THE WORRY MONSTER

Daily Doodle OR Pattern

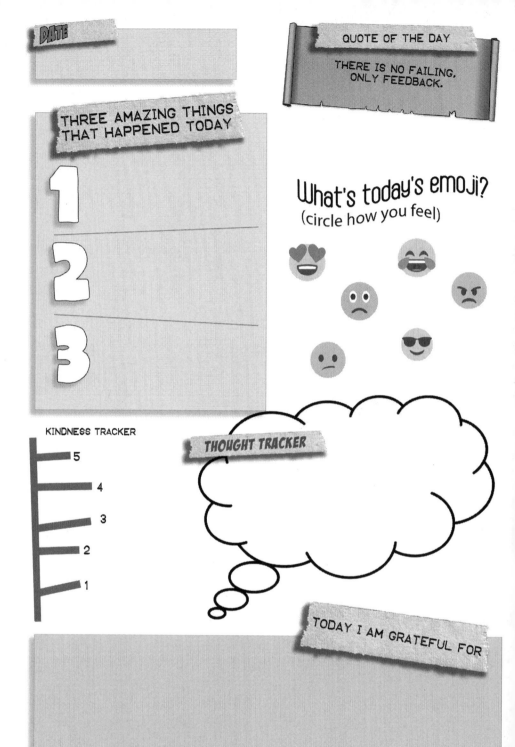

DATE

QUOTE OF THE DAY

THERE IS NO FAILING,
ONLY FEEDBACK.

THREE AMAZING THINGS
THAT HAPPENED TODAY

1

2

3

What's today's emoji?
(circle how you feel)

KINDNESS TRACKER

5

4

3

2

1

THOUGHT TRACKER

TODAY I AM GRATEFUL FOR

THE GOOD THINGS CHECKLIST

- [ ] I TIDIED SOMETHING
- [ ] I WAS A GOOD FRIEND
- [ ] I SMILED ABOUT SOMETHING
- [ ] I HELPED SOMEONE
- [ ] I HELPED MYSELF
- [ ] I TRIED MY HARDEST

Daily Doodle OR pattern

FEED THE WORRY MONSTER

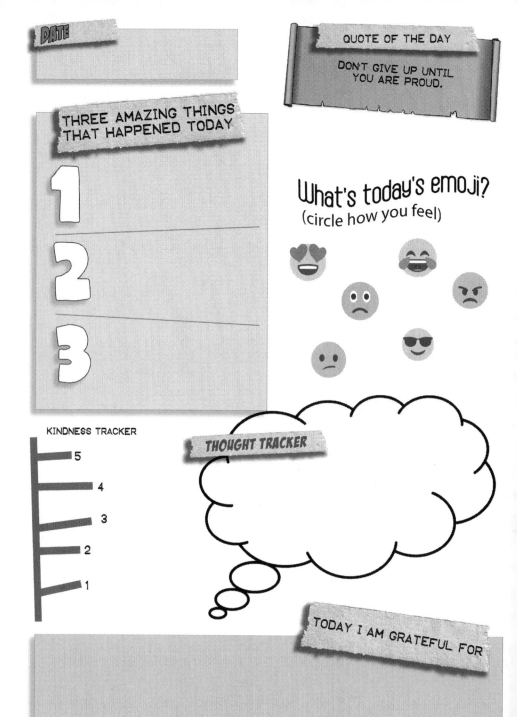

DATE

QUOTE OF THE DAY

DON'T GIVE UP UNTIL
YOU ARE PROUD.

THREE AMAZING THINGS
THAT HAPPENED TODAY

1

2

3

What's today's emoji?
(circle how you feel)

KINDNESS TRACKER

5

4

3

2

1

THOUGHT TRACKER

TODAY I AM GRATEFUL FOR

THE GOOD THINGS CHECKLIST

- ☐ I TIDIED SOMETHING
- ☐ I WAS A GOOD FRIEND
- ☐ I SMILED ABOUT SOMETHING
- ☐ I HELPED SOMEONE
- ☐ I HELPED MYSELF
- ☐ I TRIED MY HARDEST

Daily Doodle or pattern

FEED THE WORRY MONSTER

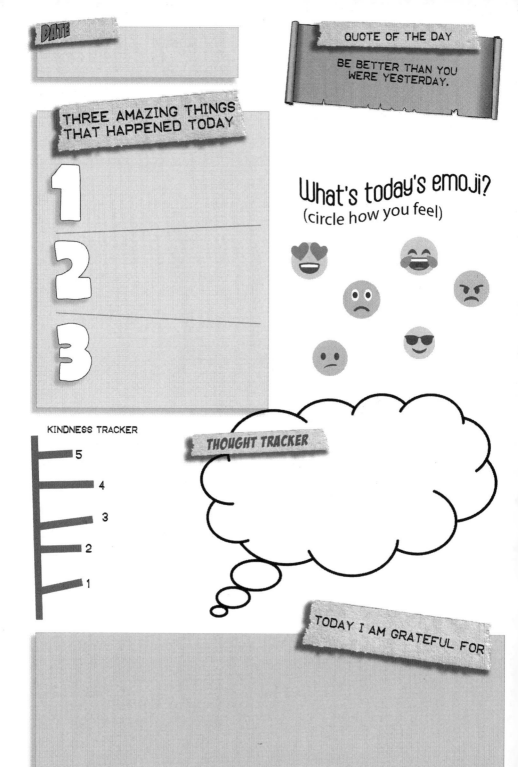

DATE

QUOTE OF THE DAY

BE BETTER THAN YOU WERE YESTERDAY.

THREE AMAZING THINGS THAT HAPPENED TODAY

1

2

3

What's today's emoji?
(circle how you feel)

KINDNESS TRACKER

5
4
3
2
1

THOUGHT TRACKER

TODAY I AM GRATEFUL FOR

THE GOOD THINGS CHECKLIST

FEED THE WORRY MONSTER

- [ ] I TIDIED SOMETHING
- [ ] I WAS A GOOD FRIEND
- [ ] I SMILED ABOUT SOMETHING
- [ ] I HELPED SOMEONE
- [ ] I HELPED MYSELF
- [ ] I TRIED MY HARDEST

Daily Doodle or Pattern

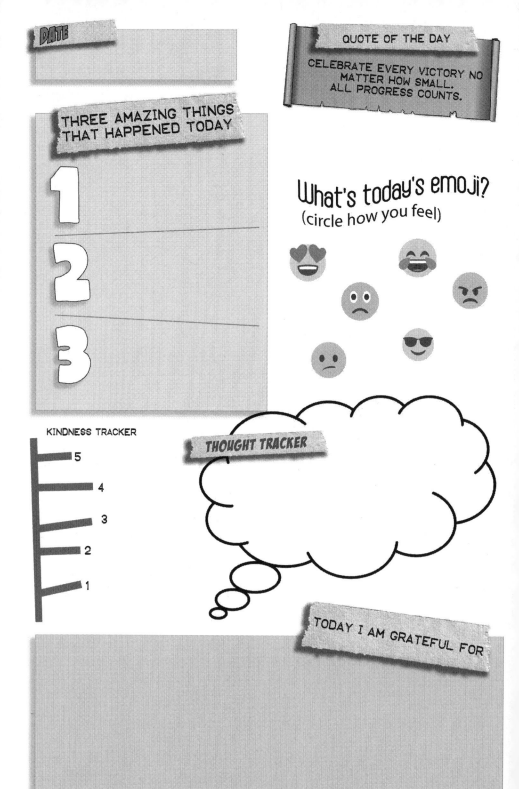

DATE

QUOTE OF THE DAY

CELEBRATE EVERY VICTORY NO MATTER HOW SMALL. ALL PROGRESS COUNTS.

THREE AMAZING THINGS THAT HAPPENED TODAY

1

2

3

What's today's emoji?
(circle how you feel)

KINDNESS TRACKER

5

4

3

2

1

THOUGHT TRACKER

TODAY I AM GRATEFUL FOR

THE GOOD THINGS CHECKLIST

- ☐ I TIDIED SOMETHING
- ☐ I WAS A GOOD FRIEND
- ☐ I SMILED ABOUT SOMETHING
- ☐ I HELPED SOMEONE
- ☐ I HELPED MYSELF
- ☐ I TRIED MY HARDEST

FEED THE WORRY MONSTER

Daily Doodle or Pattern

DATE

THREE AMAZING THINGS
THAT HAPPENED TODAY

1

2

3

What's today's emoji?
(circle how you feel)

KINDNESS TRACKER

5

4

3

2

1

THOUGHT TRACKER

TODAY I AM GRATEFUL FOR

THE GOOD THINGS CHECKLIST

FEED THE WORRY MONSTER

- ☐ I TIDIED SOMETHING
- ☐ I WAS A GOOD FRIEND
- ☐ I SMILED ABOUT SOMETHING
- ☐ I HELPED SOMEONE
- ☐ I HELPED MYSELF
- ☐ I TRIED MY HARDEST

Daily Doodle OR Pattern

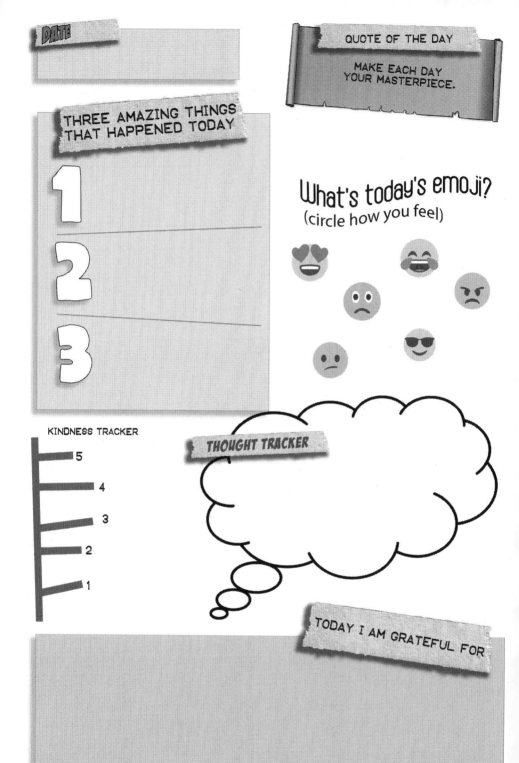

DATE

QUOTE OF THE DAY

MAKE EACH DAY
YOUR MASTERPIECE.

THREE AMAZING THINGS
THAT HAPPENED TODAY

1

2

3

What's today's emoji?
(circle how you feel)

KINDNESS TRACKER

5

4

3

2

1

THOUGHT TRACKER

TODAY I AM GRATEFUL FOR

THE GOOD THINGS CHECKLIST

- ☐ I TIDIED SOMETHING
- ☐ I WAS A GOOD FRIEND
- ☐ I SMILED ABOUT SOMETHING
- ☐ I HELPED SOMEONE
- ☐ I HELPED MYSELF
- ☐ I TRIED MY HARDEST

Daily Doodle or pattern

FEED THE WORRY MONSTER

DATE

QUOTE OF THE DAY

WE WILL EITHER FIND A WAY,
OR MAKE ONE!

THREE AMAZING THINGS
THAT HAPPENED TODAY

1

2

3

What's today's emoji?
(circle how you feel)

KINDNESS TRACKER

5

4

3

2

1

THOUGHT TRACKER

TODAY I AM GRATEFUL FOR

THE GOOD THINGS CHECKLIST

- [ ] I TIDIED SOMETHING
- [ ] I WAS A GOOD FRIEND
- [ ] I SMILED ABOUT SOMETHING
- [ ] I HELPED SOMEONE
- [ ] I HELPED MYSELF
- [ ] I TRIED MY HARDEST

Daily Doodle OR pattern

FEED THE WORRY MONSTER

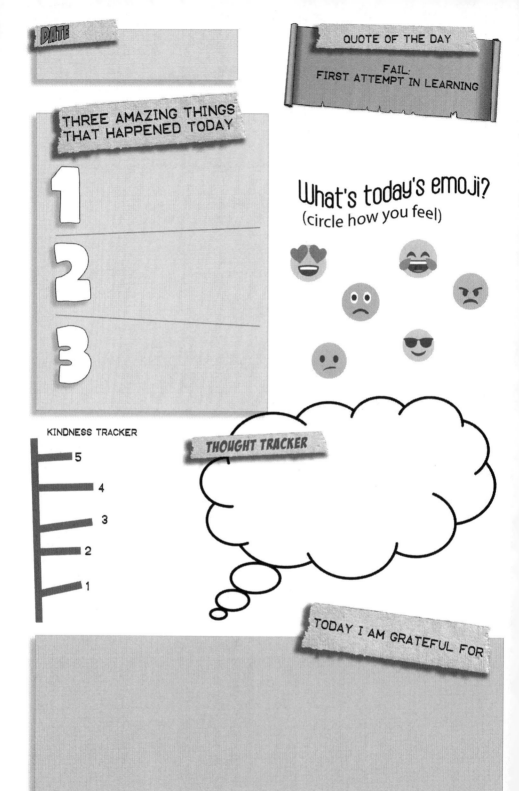

DATE

QUOTE OF THE DAY

FAIL:
FIRST ATTEMPT IN LEARNING

THREE AMAZING THINGS
THAT HAPPENED TODAY

1

2

3

What's today's emoji?
(circle how you feel)

KINDNESS TRACKER

5
4
3
2
1

THOUGHT TRACKER

TODAY I AM GRATEFUL FOR

LISTS AND BULLET JOURNAL DESIGNS

THE GOOD THINGS CHECKLIST

- [ ] I TIDIED SOMETHING
- [ ] I WAS A GOOD FRIEND
- [ ] I SMILED ABOUT SOMETHING
- [ ] I HELPED SOMEONE
- [ ] I HELPED MYSELF
- [ ] I TRIED MY HARDEST

Daily Doodle OR Pattern

FEED THE WORRY MONSTER

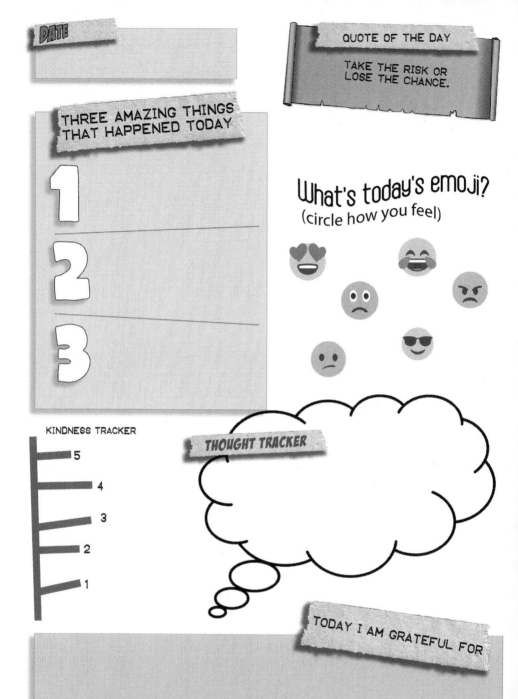

DATE

QUOTE OF THE DAY

TAKE THE RISK OR
LOSE THE CHANCE.

THREE AMAZING THINGS
THAT HAPPENED TODAY

1

2

3

What's today's emoji?
(circle how you feel)

KINDNESS TRACKER

5

4

3

2

1

THOUGHT TRACKER

TODAY I AM GRATEFUL FOR

THE GOOD THINGS CHECKLIST

FEED THE WORRY MONSTER

- [ ] I TIDIED SOMETHING
- [ ] I WAS A GOOD FRIEND
- [ ] I SMILED ABOUT SOMETHING
- [ ] I HELPED SOMEONE
- [ ] I HELPED MYSELF
- [ ] I TRIED MY HARDEST

Daily Doodle OR pattern

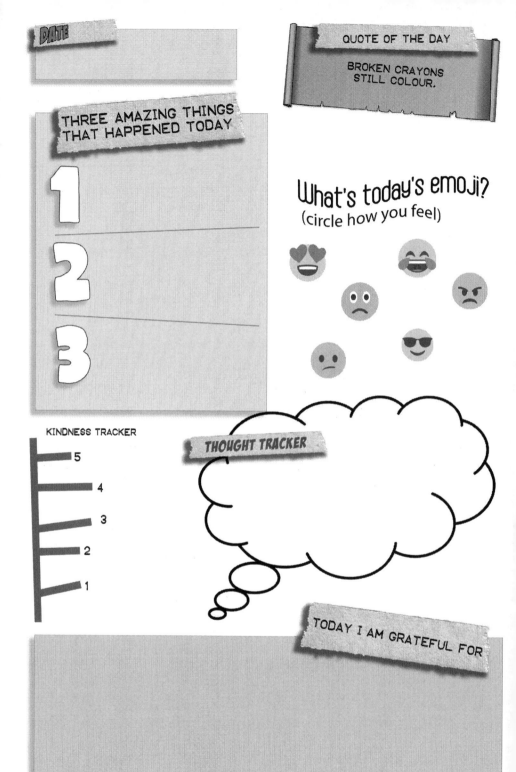

THE GOOD THINGS CHECKLIST

FEED THE WORRY MONSTER

- [ ] I TIDIED SOMETHING
- [ ] I WAS A GOOD FRIEND
- [ ] I SMILED ABOUT SOMETHING
- [ ] I HELPED SOMEONE
- [ ] I HELPED MYSELF
- [ ] I TRIED MY HARDEST

Daily Doodle OR pattern

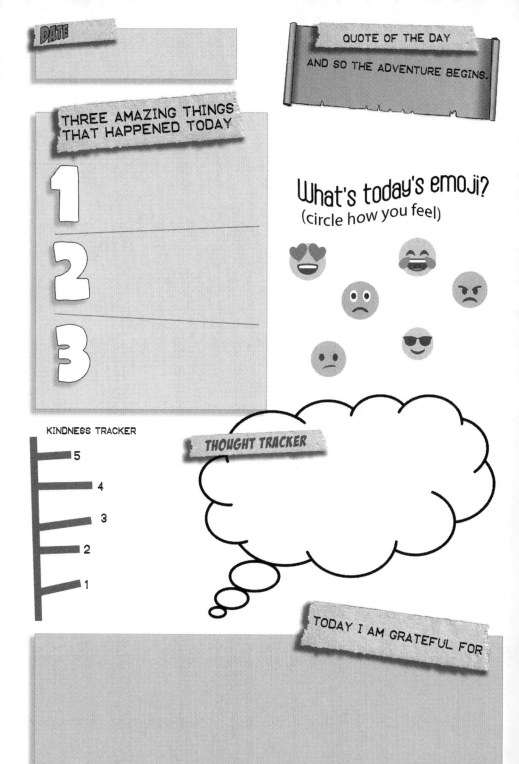

THE GOOD THINGS CHECKLIST

FEED THE WORRY MONSTER

- [ ] I TIDIED SOMETHING
- [ ] I WAS A GOOD FRIEND
- [ ] I SMILED ABOUT SOMETHING
- [ ] I HELPED SOMEONE
- [ ] I HELPED MYSELF
- [ ] I TRIED MY HARDEST

Daily Doodle OR pattern

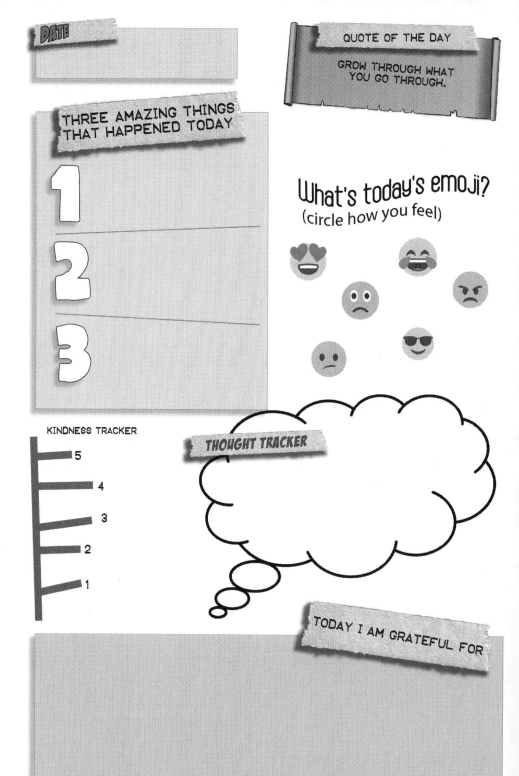

DATE

QUOTE OF THE DAY

GROW THROUGH WHAT YOU GO THROUGH.

THREE AMAZING THINGS THAT HAPPENED TODAY

1

2

3

What's today's emoji?
(circle how you feel)

KINDNESS TRACKER

5
4
3
2
1

THOUGHT TRACKER

TODAY I AM GRATEFUL FOR

THE GOOD THINGS CHECKLIST

☐ I TIDIED SOMETHING

☐ I WAS A GOOD FRIEND

☐ I SMILED ABOUT SOMETHING

☐ I HELPED SOMEONE

☐ I HELPED MYSELF

☐ I TRIED MY HARDEST

Daily Doodle OR pattern

FEED THE WORRY MONSTER

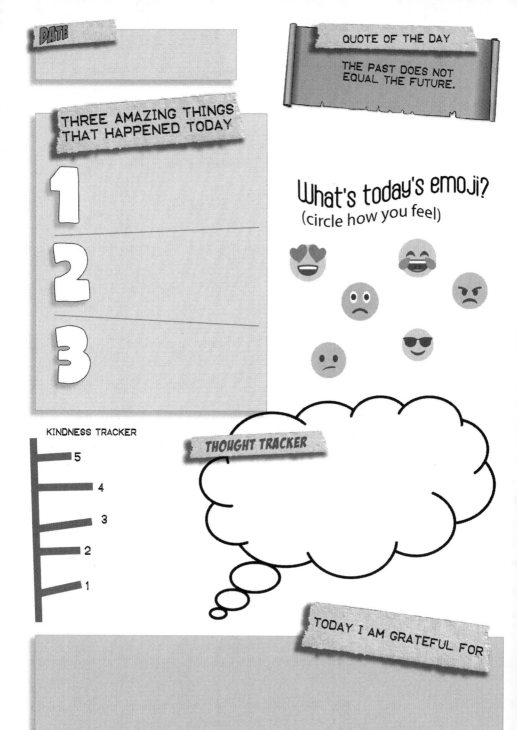

DATE

QUOTE OF THE DAY

THE PAST DOES NOT
EQUAL THE FUTURE.

THREE AMAZING THINGS
THAT HAPPENED TODAY

1

2

3

What's today's emoji?
(circle how you feel)

KINDNESS TRACKER

5

4

3

2

1

THOUGHT TRACKER

TODAY I AM GRATEFUL FOR

THE GOOD THINGS CHECKLIST

- ☐ I TIDIED SOMETHING
- ☐ I WAS A GOOD FRIEND
- ☐ I SMILED ABOUT SOMETHING
- ☐ I HELPED SOMEONE
- ☐ I HELPED MYSELF
- ☐ I TRIED MY HARDEST

FEED THE WORRY MONSTER

Daily Doodle or pattern

DATE

THREE AMAZING THINGS
THAT HAPPENED TODAY

1

2

3

What's today's emoji?
(circle how you feel)

KINDNESS TRACKER

5

4

3

2

1

THOUGHT TRACKER

TODAY I AM GRATEFUL FOR

THE GOOD THINGS CHECKLIST

FEED THE WORRY MONSTER

- [ ] I TIDIED SOMETHING
- [ ] I WAS A GOOD FRIEND
- [ ] I SMILED ABOUT SOMETHING
- [ ] I HELPED SOMEONE
- [ ] I HELPED MYSELF
- [ ] I TRIED MY HARDEST

Daily Doodle or pattern

DATE

THREE AMAZING THINGS
THAT HAPPENED TODAY

1

2

3

What's today's emoji?
(circle how you feel)

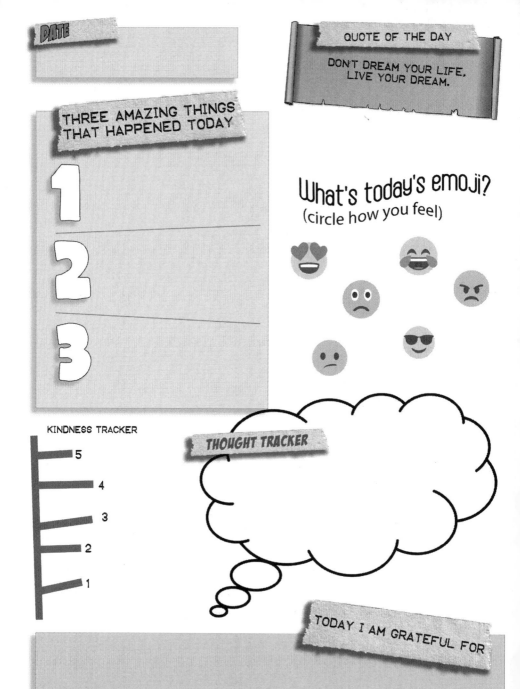

KINDNESS TRACKER

5
4
3
2
1

THOUGHT TRACKER

TODAY I AM GRATEFUL FOR

THE GOOD THINGS CHECKLIST

- ☐ I TIDIED SOMETHING
- ☐ I WAS A GOOD FRIEND
- ☐ I SMILED ABOUT SOMETHING
- ☐ I HELPED SOMEONE
- ☐ I HELPED MYSELF
- ☐ I TRIED MY HARDEST

Daily Doodle or Pattern

FEED THE WORRY MONSTER

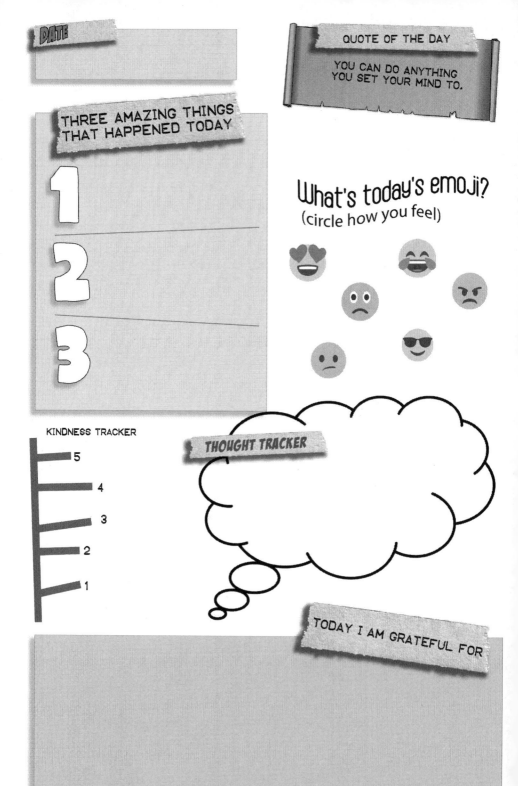

DATE

QUOTE OF THE DAY

YOU CAN DO ANYTHING
YOU SET YOUR MIND TO.

THREE AMAZING THINGS
THAT HAPPENED TODAY

1

2

3

What's today's emoji?
(circle how you feel)

KINDNESS TRACKER

5
4
3
2
1

THOUGHT TRACKER

TODAY I AM GRATEFUL FOR

THE GOOD THINGS CHECKLIST

- ☐ I TIDIED SOMETHING
- ☐ I WAS A GOOD FRIEND
- ☐ I SMILED ABOUT SOMETHING
- ☐ I HELPED SOMEONE
- ☐ I HELPED MYSELF
- ☐ I TRIED MY HARDEST

Daily Doodle OR Pattern

FEED THE WORRY MONSTER

DATE

QUOTE OF THE DAY

ACTUALLY, YOU CAN.

THREE AMAZING THINGS
THAT HAPPENED TODAY

1

2

3

What's today's emoji?
(circle how you feel)

KINDNESS TRACKER

5
4
3
2
1

THOUGHT TRACKER

TODAY I AM GRATEFUL FOR

THE GOOD THINGS CHECKLIST

FEED THE WORRY MONSTER

- ☐ I TIDIED SOMETHING
- ☐ I WAS A GOOD FRIEND
- ☐ I SMILED ABOUT SOMETHING
- ☐ I HELPED SOMEONE
- ☐ I HELPED MYSELF
- ☐ I TRIED MY HARDEST

Daily Doodle OR pattern

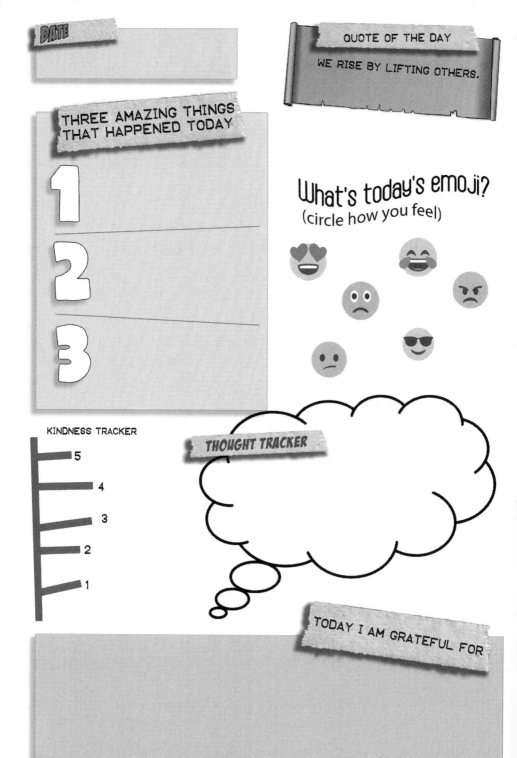

DATE

QUOTE OF THE DAY

WE RISE BY LIFTING OTHERS.

THREE AMAZING THINGS THAT HAPPENED TODAY

1

2

3

What's today's emoji?
(circle how you feel)

KINDNESS TRACKER

5
4
3
2
1

THOUGHT TRACKER

TODAY I AM GRATEFUL FOR

THE GOOD THINGS CHECKLIST

- ☐ I TIDIED SOMETHING
- ☐ I WAS A GOOD FRIEND
- ☐ I SMILED ABOUT SOMETHING
- ☐ I HELPED SOMEONE
- ☐ I HELPED MYSELF
- ☐ I TRIED MY HARDEST

Daily Doodle OR pattern

FEED THE WORRY MONSTER

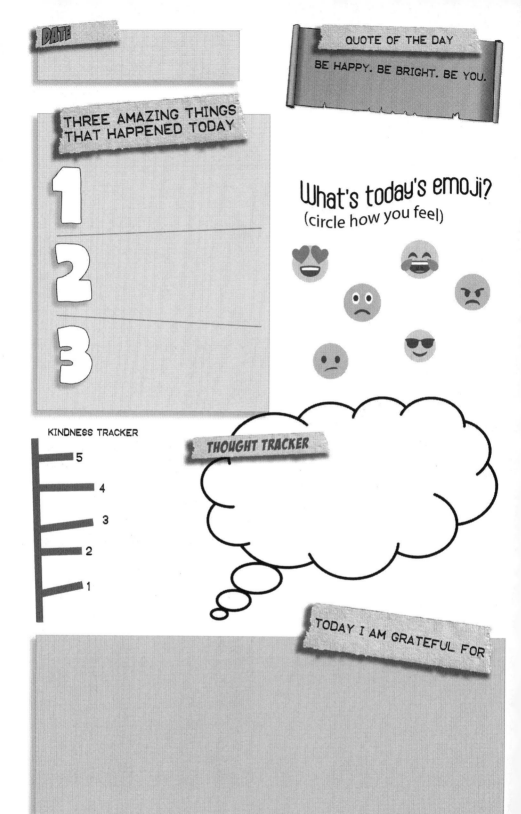

DATE

QUOTE OF THE DAY

BE HAPPY. BE BRIGHT. BE YOU.

THREE AMAZING THINGS
THAT HAPPENED TODAY

1

2

3

What's today's emoji?
(circle how you feel)

KINDNESS TRACKER

5

4

3

2

1

THOUGHT TRACKER

TODAY I AM GRATEFUL FOR

THE GOOD THINGS CHECKLIST

- ☐ I TIDIED SOMETHING
- ☐ I WAS A GOOD FRIEND
- ☐ I SMILED ABOUT SOMETHING
- ☐ I HELPED SOMEONE
- ☐ I HELPED MYSELF
- ☐ I TRIED MY HARDEST

Daily Doodle or pattern

FEED THE WORRY MONSTER

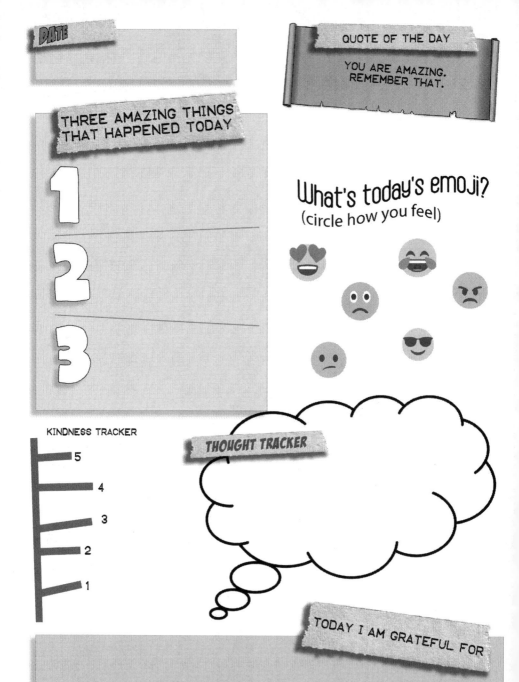

DATE

QUOTE OF THE DAY

YOU ARE AMAZING.
REMEMBER THAT.

THREE AMAZING THINGS
THAT HAPPENED TODAY

1

2

3

What's today's emoji?
(circle how you feel)

KINDNESS TRACKER

5

4

3

2

1

THOUGHT TRACKER

TODAY I AM GRATEFUL FOR

THE GOOD THINGS CHECKLIST

FEED THE WORRY MONSTER

☐ I TIDIED SOMETHING

☐ I WAS A GOOD FRIEND

☐ I SMILED ABOUT SOMETHING

☐ I HELPED SOMEONE

☐ I HELPED MYSELF

☐ I TRIED MY HARDEST

Daily Doodle OR Pattern

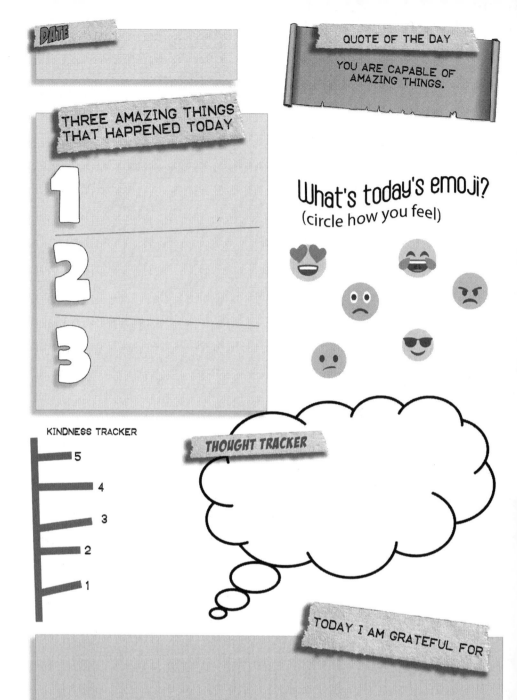

DATE

QUOTE OF THE DAY

YOU ARE CAPABLE OF
AMAZING THINGS.

THREE AMAZING THINGS
THAT HAPPENED TODAY

1

2

3

What's today's emoji?
(circle how you feel)

KINDNESS TRACKER

5

4

3

2

1

THOUGHT TRACKER

TODAY I AM GRATEFUL FOR

THE GOOD THINGS CHECKLIST

FEED THE WORRY MONSTER

- ☐ I TIDIED SOMETHING
- ☐ I WAS A GOOD FRIEND
- ☐ I SMILED ABOUT SOMETHING
- ☐ I HELPED SOMEONE
- ☐ I HELPED MYSELF
- ☐ I TRIED MY HARDEST

Daily Doodle OR pattern

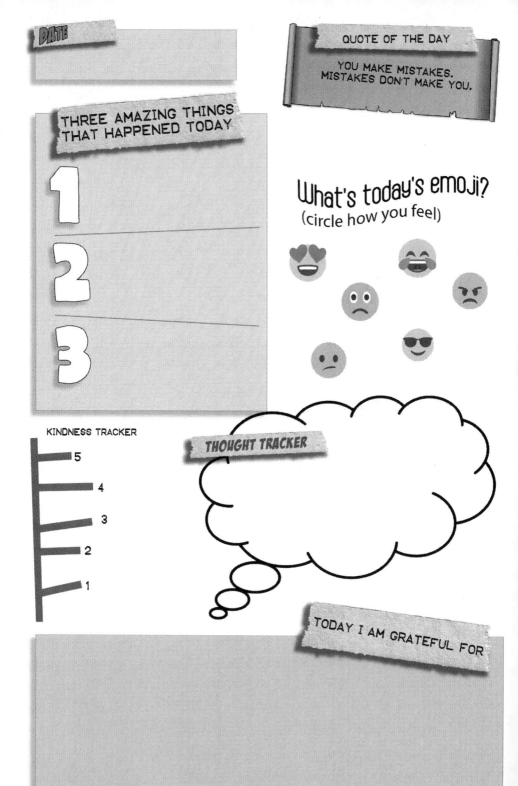

DATE

QUOTE OF THE DAY

YOU MAKE MISTAKES.
MISTAKES DON'T MAKE YOU.

THREE AMAZING THINGS
THAT HAPPENED TODAY

1

2

3

What's today's emoji?
(circle how you feel)

KINDNESS TRACKER

5

4

3

2

1

THOUGHT TRACKER

TODAY I AM GRATEFUL FOR

THE GOOD THINGS CHECKLIST

- [ ] I TIDIED SOMETHING
- [ ] I WAS A GOOD FRIEND
- [ ] I SMILED ABOUT SOMETHING
- [ ] I HELPED SOMEONE
- [ ] I HELPED MYSELF
- [ ] I TRIED MY HARDEST

Daily Doodle OR Pattern

FEED THE WORRY MONSTER

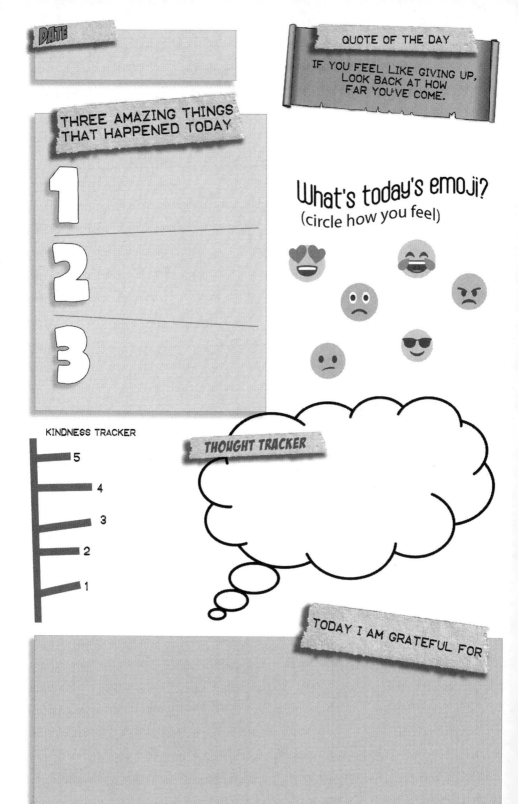

DATE

QUOTE OF THE DAY

IF YOU FEEL LIKE GIVING UP,
LOOK BACK AT HOW
FAR YOU'VE COME.

THREE AMAZING THINGS
THAT HAPPENED TODAY

1

2

3

What's today's emoji?
(circle how you feel)

KINDNESS TRACKER

5
4
3
2
1

THOUGHT TRACKER

TODAY I AM GRATEFUL FOR

THE GOOD THINGS
CHECKLIST

FEED THE WORRY MONSTER

- [ ] I TIDIED SOMETHING
- [ ] I WAS A GOOD FRIEND
- [ ] I SMILED ABOUT SOMETHING
- [ ] I HELPED SOMEONE
- [ ] I HELPED MYSELF
- [ ] I TRIED MY HARDEST

Daily Doodle or pattern

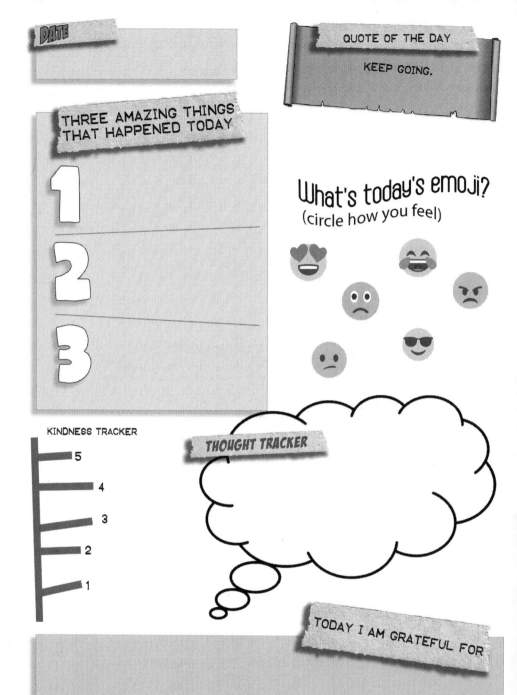

DATE

THREE AMAZING THINGS THAT HAPPENED TODAY

1

2

3

What's today's emoji?
(circle how you feel)

KINDNESS TRACKER

5

4

3

2

1

THOUGHT TRACKER

TODAY I AM GRATEFUL FOR

THE GOOD THINGS CHECKLIST

- [ ] I TIDIED SOMETHING
- [ ] I WAS A GOOD FRIEND
- [ ] I SMILED ABOUT SOMETHING
- [ ] I HELPED SOMEONE
- [ ] I HELPED MYSELF
- [ ] I TRIED MY HARDEST

Daily Doodle OR Pattern

FEED THE WORRY MONSTER

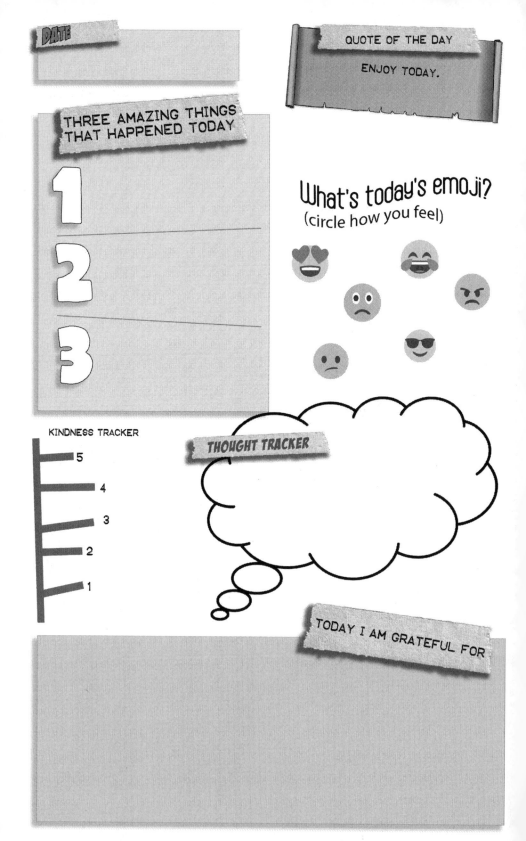

DATE

THREE AMAZING THINGS
THAT HAPPENED TODAY

1

2

3

What's today's emoji?
(circle how you feel)

KINDNESS TRACKER

5

4

3

2

1

THOUGHT TRACKER

TODAY I AM GRATEFUL FOR

THE GOOD THINGS CHECKLIST

- [ ] I TIDIED SOMETHING
- [ ] I WAS A GOOD FRIEND
- [ ] I SMILED ABOUT SOMETHING
- [ ] I HELPED SOMEONE
- [ ] I HELPED MYSELF
- [ ] I TRIED MY HARDEST

Daily Doodle OR Pattern

FEED THE WORRY MONSTER

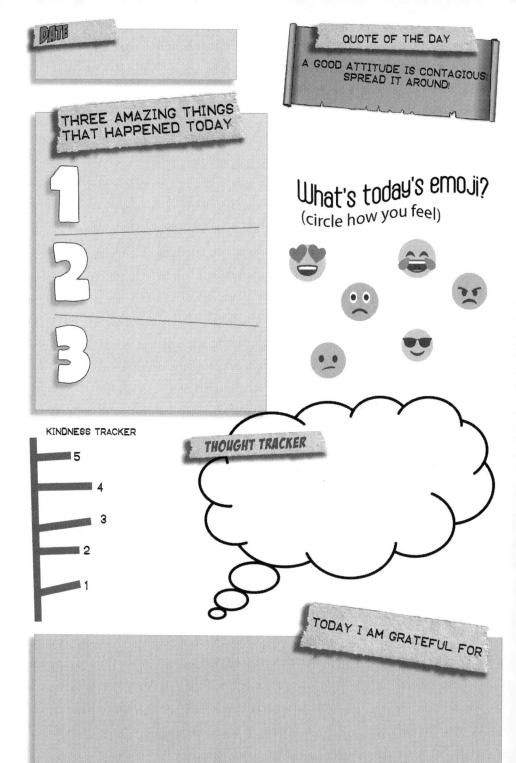

THE GOOD THINGS CHECKLIST

- [ ] I TIDIED SOMETHING
- [ ] I WAS A GOOD FRIEND
- [ ] I SMILED ABOUT SOMETHING
- [ ] I HELPED SOMEONE
- [ ] I HELPED MYSELF
- [ ] I TRIED MY HARDEST

Daily Doodle or Pattern

FEED THE WORRY MONSTER

THREE AMAZING THINGS THAT HAPPENED TODAY

1

2

3

What's today's emoji?
(circle how you feel)

KINDNESS TRACKER

5

4

3

2

1

THOUGHT TRACKER

TODAY I AM GRATEFUL FOR

THE GOOD THINGS CHECKLIST

- [ ] I TIDIED SOMETHING
- [ ] I WAS A GOOD FRIEND
- [ ] I SMILED ABOUT SOMETHING
- [ ] I HELPED SOMEONE
- [ ] I HELPED MYSELF
- [ ] I TRIED MY HARDEST

Daily Doodle OR Pattern

FEED THE WORRY MONSTER

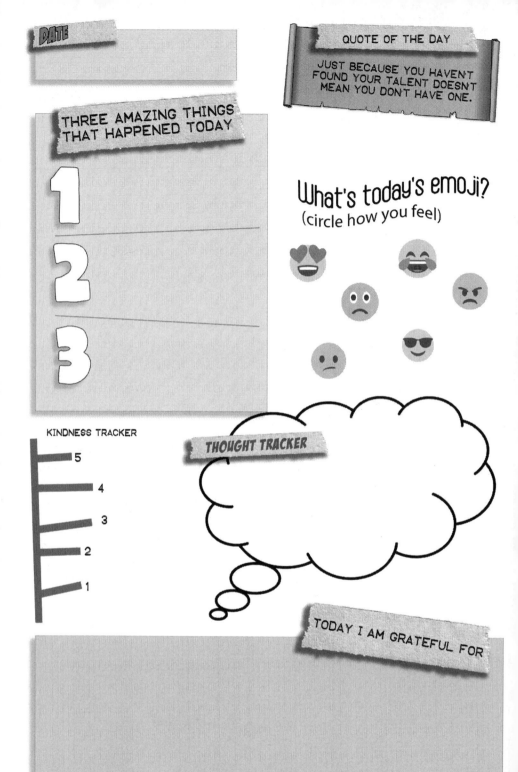

DATE

QUOTE OF THE DAY

JUST BECAUSE YOU HAVEN'T FOUND YOUR TALENT DOESN'T MEAN YOU DON'T HAVE ONE.

THREE AMAZING THINGS THAT HAPPENED TODAY

1

2

3

What's today's emoji?
(circle how you feel)

KINDNESS TRACKER

5
4
3
2
1

THOUGHT TRACKER

TODAY I AM GRATEFUL FOR

THE GOOD THINGS CHECKLIST

- [ ] I TIDIED SOMETHING
- [ ] I WAS A GOOD FRIEND
- [ ] I SMILED ABOUT SOMETHING
- [ ] I HELPED SOMEONE
- [ ] I HELPED MYSELF
- [ ] I TRIED MY HARDEST

Daily Doodle OR pattern

FEED THE WORRY MONSTER

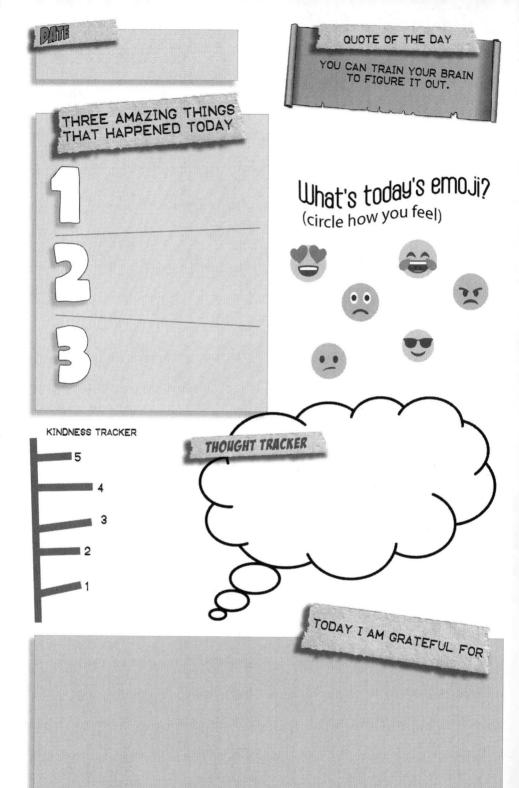

DATE

THREE AMAZING THINGS
THAT HAPPENED TODAY

1

2

3

What's today's emoji?
(circle how you feel)

KINDNESS TRACKER

5

4

3

2

1

THOUGHT TRACKER

TODAY I AM GRATEFUL FOR

THE GOOD THINGS CHECKLIST

- ☐ I TIDIED SOMETHING
- ☐ I WAS A GOOD FRIEND
- ☐ I SMILED ABOUT SOMETHING
- ☐ I HELPED SOMEONE
- ☐ I HELPED MYSELF
- ☐ I TRIED MY HARDEST

Daily Doodle OR Pattern

FEED THE WORRY MONSTER

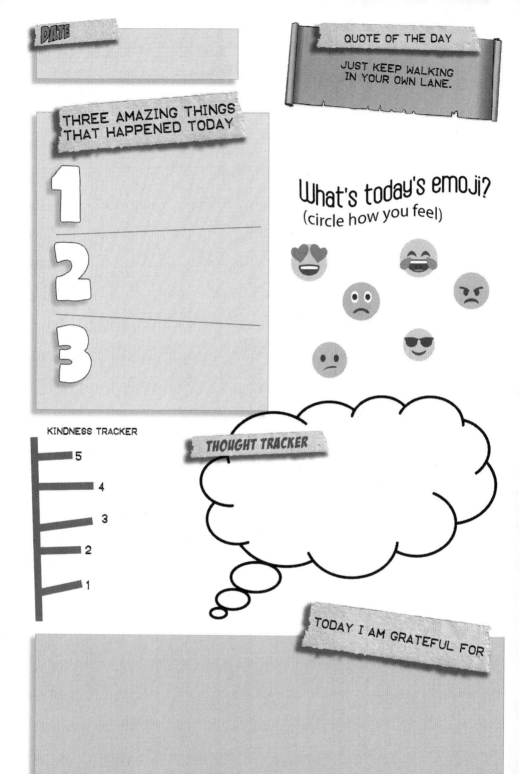

THE GOOD THINGS CHECKLIST

- [ ] I TIDIED SOMETHING
- [ ] I WAS A GOOD FRIEND
- [ ] I SMILED ABOUT SOMETHING
- [ ] I HELPED SOMEONE
- [ ] I HELPED MYSELF
- [ ] I TRIED MY HARDEST

FEED THE WORRY MONSTER

Daily Doodle or pattern

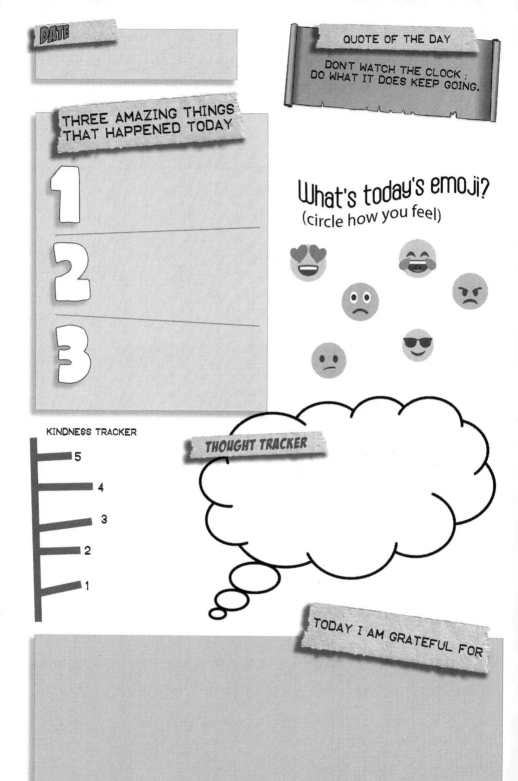

DATE

QUOTE OF THE DAY

DON'T WATCH THE CLOCK ;
DO WHAT IT DOES KEEP GOING.

THREE AMAZING THINGS
THAT HAPPENED TODAY

1

2

3

What's today's emoji?
(circle how you feel)

KINDNESS TRACKER

5
4
3
2
1

THOUGHT TRACKER

TODAY I AM GRATEFUL FOR

THE GOOD THINGS CHECKLIST

- [ ] I TIDIED SOMETHING
- [ ] I WAS A GOOD FRIEND
- [ ] I SMILED ABOUT SOMETHING
- [ ] I HELPED SOMEONE
- [ ] I HELPED MYSELF
- [ ] I TRIED MY HARDEST

Daily Doodle OR Pattern

FEED THE WORRY MONSTER

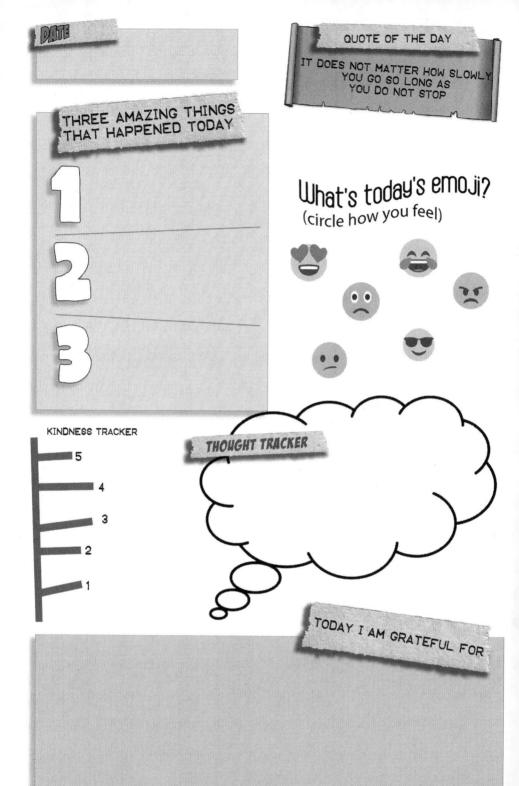

DATE

THREE AMAZING THINGS
THAT HAPPENED TODAY

1

2

3

What's today's emoji?
(circle how you feel)

KINDNESS TRACKER

5

4

3

2

1

THOUGHT TRACKER

TODAY I AM GRATEFUL FOR

THE GOOD THINGS
CHECKLIST

- ☐ I TIDIED SOMETHING
- ☐ I WAS A GOOD FRIEND
- ☐ I SMILED ABOUT SOMETHING
- ☐ I HELPED SOMEONE
- ☐ I HELPED MYSELF
- ☐ I TRIED MY HARDEST

Daily Doodle or pattern

FEED THE WORRY MONSTER

DATE

QUOTE OF THE DAY

NEVER STOP TRYING!

THREE AMAZING THINGS
THAT HAPPENED TODAY

1

2

3

What's today's emoji?
(circle how you feel)

KINDNESS TRACKER

5

4

3

2

1

THOUGHT TRACKER

TODAY I AM GRATEFUL FOR

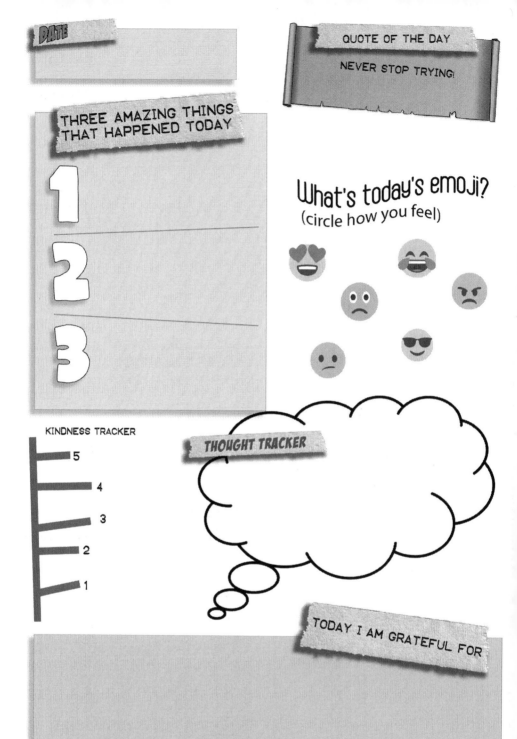

THE GOOD THINGS CHECKLIST

FEED THE WORRY MONSTER

- ☐ I TIDIED SOMETHING
- ☐ I WAS A GOOD FRIEND
- ☐ I SMILED ABOUT SOMETHING
- ☐ I HELPED SOMEONE
- ☐ I HELPED MYSELF
- ☐ I TRIED MY HARDEST

Daily Doodle or Pattern

about the artist

This book was created by artist Steve 'Squidoodle' Turner. A published illustrator of over 12 colouring books, tattoo books and journals, he also created all the drawings throughout this journal . To see more of Steve's work, follow him on facebook:

www.facebook.com/SquidDoodleArt

and on instagram:

www.instagram.com/squidoodleart

For all of Steve's other books on Amazon, search for **'Squidoodle'.**

I'd like to thank the following people for contributing daily quotes:

Anna Burke
Sarah Sanders
Kerry Witts Nearly Moseley
Amy Manchester
Pip Goodwin
Nancy Haarbrink-van Der Werf
Sam Critchley
Emma Carrington
Hannah Filer
Cheryl Boehm
Claire Chandler
Lynette Hansen-McNamara
Ryo Ryan
Gaylene Stains
Missi Mishko
Geraldine Herbert
Mhairi Shewan
Teresa Sharkey
Anna Jensen
Natasha Lewis
Jaymie Lee
Amanda Mercer
Launa Hardy
Caz DeFazio
Gabby Ball
Sarah Louise Smith
Jane Myles
Lori Hollander McHugh
Laura-Anne Sutcliffe
Gillian Susan Lloyd
Esther Nicolaou
Alison Flora
Kelli Sandison
Ellen Beth Hogg

Manufactured by Amazon.ca
Bolton, ON

22068708R00122